Dinah Livingstone is a poet, trans
magazine *Sofia*. She has received t
awards for her poetry and ran the
for twenty years. She lives in Lond

BY DINAH LIVINGSTONE
Poetry Books:
Kindness (2007)
Presence (2003)
Time on Earth: Selected and New Poems (1999)
May Day (1997)
Second Sight (1993)
Keeping Heart (1989)
Saving Grace (1987)
Poetry Pamphlets:
St Pancras Wells (1991)
Something Understood (1985)
Glad Rags (1983)
Love in Time (1982)
Prepositions and Conjunctions (1977)
Ultrasound (1974)
Maranatha (1969)
Tohu Bohu (1968)
Beginning (1967)
Prose:
The Poetry of Earth (2000)
Poetry Handbook for Readers and Writers (1992)
Edited:
This Life on Earth (prose and poetry 2009)
Work: An Anthology (prose and poetry 1999)
Camden Voices Anthology 1978–1990 (poetry 1990)
Her Translations Include:
Poetry:
Nosotras: Poems by Nicaraguan Women (trans. & ed.); Daisy Zamora, *Life for Each; Poets of the Nicaraguan Revolution* (trans. & ed.); María Eugenia Bravo Calderara, *Prayer in the National Stadium;* Ernesto Cardenal, *The Music of the Spheres;* Carlos & Luis Enrique Mejía Godoy and Julio Valle-Castillo, *The Nicaraguan Epic;* Roberto Rivera-Reyes, *Dawn Hunters and other Poems* (part); *Anthology of Latin American Poets in London* (part); Ernesto Cardenal, *Nicaraguan New Time;* Carlos Mejía Godoy, *Nicaraguan Mass (Misa Campesina);* Lorca and John of the Cross, *Poems.*
Prose:
Jon Sobrino, *The Eye of the Needle;* Nestor-Luis Cordero, *By Being, It Is: The Thesis of Parmenides;* Subcomandante Marcos, *Zapatista Stories;* Kintto Lucas, *We Will Not Dance on our Grandparents' Tombs: Indigenous Uprisings in Ecuador;* Anselm Grün, *Angels of Grace;* Tomás Borge, *Carlos, Now the Dawn's No Fond Illusion;* María Pilar Aquino, *Our Cry for Life;* Luis Alonso Schökel, *Moses;* Jon Sobrino, *Companions of Jesus: The Murder and Martyrdom of the Salvadorean Jesuits;* Jon Sobrino, *The Crucified Peoples;* M. López Vigil, *Death and Life in Morazán;* Walter Beyerlin, *We are like Dreamers;* A. Pérez Esclarín, *Jesús of Gramoven;* Ernesto Cardenal, *Love;* Helder Camara, *The Desert is Fertile;* Alain Labrousse, *The Tupamaros;* Wilhelm Weitling, *The Poor Sinner's Gospel;* Dorothee Sölle, *The Truth is Concrete;* Georg Schäfer, *In the Kingdom of Mescal;* Karl Rahner, *Nature and Grace.*

POETIC TALES

POETIC TALES

Logosofia Down to Earth

Dinah Livingstone

KATABASIS

First published on 19th July 2010
by KATABASIS
10 St Martin's Close, London NW1 0HR (020 7485 3830)
katabasis@katabasis.co.uk
www.katabasis.co.uk
Copyright © Dinah Livingstone 2010
Designed and typeset in-house mainly in 12 point Garamond.
Printed in England by imprint**digital**.net
Front cover painting: Anne Mieke Lumsden
Frontispiece: 'The Son Offers to Redeem Humanity', illustration to
Paradise Lost by William Blake

ISBN: 978-0-904872-44-6
Trade Distribution: Central Books
99 Wallis Road
London E9 5LN
Telephone: 44 (0)845 458 9911

British Library Cataloguing in Publication Data:
A catalogue record for this book is available
from the British Library.

Contents

Acknowledgments

Parts of this book in earlier versions have been given as talks in London and Oxford, and published as articles in the *Ethical Record* and *Sofia*.

Heartfelt thanks to those who have read, criticised and/or proof-read the book: Kelly Walker, Kathleen McPhilemy, Francis McDonagh, Zoe and Grace Livingstone.

Forewords

Luke:

Didn't our hearts burn while he talked to us on the road?[1]

Athanasius:

The Word of God became human so that we might become God.[2]

Samuel Taylor Coleridge:

A male and female tiger is neither more nor less whether you suppose them only existing in their appropriate wilderness, or whether you suppose a thousand pairs. But man is truly altered by the co-existence of other men; his faculties cannot be developed in himself alone, and only himself. Therefore the human race, not by a bold metaphor, but in sublime reality, approach to and might become one body whose head is Christ (the Logos).[3]

William Blake:

The ancient Poets animated all sensible objects with Gods or Geniuses, calling them by the names and adorning them with the properties of woods, rivers, mountains, lakes, cities, nations, and whatever their enlarged and numerous senses could perceive.

---

[1] Lk 24: 32.
[2] Athanasius, *On the Incarnation,* 54.
[3] Coleridge, Letters III, p. 482, quoted by Richard Holmes in *Coleridge, Darker Reflections* (Flamingo, London 1998), p. 73.

1

And particularly they studied the genius of each city and country, placing it under its mental deity;

Till a system was formed, which some took advantage of, and enslaved the vulgar by attempting to realise or abstract the mental deities from their objects: thus began Priesthood;

Choosing forms of worship from poetic tales.

And at length they pronounced that the Gods had ordered such things.

Thus men forgot that All deities reside in the human breast.[4]

---

[4]   William Blake, *The Marriage of Heaven and Hell*, plate 11.

Introduction

There are probably many people like myself in Britain and elsewhere (who may or may not go to church) who regard the whole supernatural realm of God or gods, angels and demons as the rich product of the human imagination, or poetic genius as Blake called it. That view is a scandal to fundamentalists and mere foolishness to secularists who passionately loathe religion, but to me and I suspect many others, common sense. For, once we have discarded the supernatural and ask what value such 'poetic tales' can still have for us, the surprising answer is as much as ever. Not only does everyone, atheist or otherwise, need some theology, without which so much of our history and culture remains baffling, but when taken and sifted with what Coleridge called 'the willing suspension of disbelief, for the moment, which constitutes poetic faith', those tales are found to contain treasures of wisdom.

For more than twenty years Coleridge mulled over a grand over-arching work on poetry, philosophy, theology etc to be called *Logosophia:* 'Word Wisdom'. For one reason or another, being Coleridge, he never got round to it, although many of his insights subsequently appeared in his *Biographia Literaria.*[5] My book is not, of course, the one Coleridge would have written. Although its scope has a dash of Coleridgean ambition, it is more a train of thought than a treatise, sketching a twenty-first-century *Logosofia,* that combines a defence of poetry, a natural theology (with nothing supernatural about it) and a quest for kindness. After a chapter

---

[5] S.T. Coleridge's autobiographical prose work *Biographia Literaria* was a kind of prelude to his unwritten *Logosophia,* just as Wordsworth's book-length autobiographical poem, *The Prelude,* was intended as a prelude to his projected all-embracing poem *The Recluse,* which also never got written.

on the necessity of poetry, the book explores the central Christian story, not in order to add to the immense corpus of scholarship, but to ponder its enduring, purely natural, meaning and power.

My title bows to Blake, who said we 'choose forms of worship from poetic tales'. And with a curtsey to Coleridge, my subtitle is *Logosofia Down to Earth*. For the last six years I have edited the magazine *Sofia*.[6] During this time I have learnt from my authors, read and thought more, and had many conversations. So that was another reason for subtitling this little book *Logosofia Down to Earth*.

The Greek word *Logosofia* may put people off as highbrow or high-faluting, which why the second part of the subtitle is *Down to Earth*. Because we are embodied beings living on a body revolving in space, Planet Earth, whose voice we are, our poetry, word and wisdom must be earthy, embodied, incarnate. Just as poetry fleshes out, embodies and *earths* abstract ideas, the divine Word Wisdom in the Christian story comes down, 'empties itself' into flesh and blood.[7] The name *Logosofia* incorporates both the masculine Greek word *logos* and the feminine Greek word *sofia*.[8] As embodied beings, we are either male or female. Humanity requires *both* and so does its word and its wisdom.

---

[6]   *Sofia* is the magazine of the Sea of Faith – SOF – Network (Britain). www.sofn.org.uk/sofia/index.html

[7]   In the words of the statement of the Council of Nicea (325): κατελθοντα, σαρκωθεντα 'ενανθρωπησαντα *(katelthonta, sarkothenta, enanthropesanta):* 'come down, become flesh, become human'. See pages 109–10.

[8]   Christ is called both *logos* (e.g. Jn 1: 1) and *sofia* (e.g. 1 Cor 1: 24) but not combined in the one word *Logosofia,* which was probably Coleridge's own invention.

The other day I was watching my two-year-old grandson do a small wooden jigsaw of a vixen and her cub. He gradually managed to fit in all the pieces except the last, an awkward one. He tried it one way and it would not go in. Then his face lit up, he turned it the other way round and it neatly clicked into place. Done it! There is a special form of insight when we suddenly realise we have been looking at something the wrong way round or upside down. When we look at it in the new way it is the *same* – in this case the same wooden piece – but *different*. I thought such an important insight should have a name and decided to call it an Other Way Round insight.

Other Way Round insights have played a crucial part in our history. One such insight was the consciousness-shift people had to negotiate when, after millennia of certainty that the sun moves round the Earth, Galileo showed and his successors eventually convinced them that in fact the reverse was the case: the Earth moves round the sun.

We could also give a psychological example of an Other Way Round insight. If a child is tormented and hurt and made to feel bad by a parent or step parent, the child may well feel *she* is bad. But with luck when she grows up, she will one day realise it was the other way round: not she but the abusive parent was bad for being so cruel to her as a child. Or we could give a political example when a people realises that it is not their king or ruler who gives them their power and legitimacy; he gets his power and legitimacy from *them* – their ingenuity, their labour, their muscle.

Likewise today, after millennia of believing that God (or gods) created human beings, we – some of us – have realised that in fact the reverse is the case: we created God and all the gods. Nevertheless, we still experience sunrise and sunset and the poetry that expresses these events in terms of a now-superseded science can still move us. The same is true of the 'poetic tales' of God and other gods.

However, people today are often wary of poetry and theology, perhaps for the same reason: they fear 'the holiness of the heart's affections and the truth of imagination' may be a kind of trick. They think that 'fairy stories' are for children, something adults should grow out of. They think the only 'proper' truth is *prose*: something that can be established as a scientific fact. Perhaps this wariness of poetry accounts not only for the growth of rationalism, on the one hand, but also for the growth of fundamentalism, on the other. Fundamentalists assert that religious truths are *prose*. That is why they engage in endless arguments about the six days of creation, the resurrection etc. Respecting poetry and theology as sister arts, this book offers a way into poetry even for the prosaic or merely puzzled, and a way into theology for atheists and all.

The book starts by looking at the value of poetry – both poems as such and what in the more general sense we call 'poetic', 'pure poetry', the oomph of life. It explores the idea of 'poetic faith'. Arguing that poetry is not only valuable but necessary, the first chapter is called 'The Necessity of Poetry'.

The remaining three chapters (2, 3 and 4) focus on the poetic tales of the Christian story, assuming these are just one of the countless creations of the human poetic genius or imagination, but a very important one. Chapter 2, 'Mother and Father', looks at how we have created goddesses and gods to express the wonders of the world that gave birth to us – which we did not create – and our relationship to it. Chapter 3, 'Earthchild: The Making of Humanity', looks at Jesus' preaching of the kingdom of God, and at the Christ Epic as stories about what would constitute the fulfilment, the making of humanity. Then it considers the theology of the Incarnate

Word – God becoming human in Jesus Christ. Chapter 4, 'Human Kindness', asks what kind of creatures humans are, what we mean by the spirit of kindness and humanity, and considers how far we have got as a species in that direction.

It will be seen that these three chapters form a trinity, related to the trinity of the Christian God – Father, Son and Spirit – a supreme creation of the human imagination and an image of what Earth's humanity might become. More about this will emerge in the course of the book.

Chapter 1

The Necessity of Poetry

Living on Earth

Human beings are an animal species that has evolved within the ecosystem of Planet Earth. Like other animals, in order to live, we have to engage physically with our environment and one another. We are material bodies that need material things in order to survive – warmth, food, drink – and Earth is the habitat we have in which to get them. If we fail, we die. The Earth is a physical body in space and although it has been modified over the millennia by human labour, we did not create it. It is an exhaustible physical treasury given to us. Likewise, each human being that is born is given a particular, limited, mortal body. How that little body develops depends partly on his or her given genetic material and partly on how well it is looked after by parents and others.

In order to satisfy their needs, humans have developed skills in hunting, gathering, agriculture, building, carpentry, cooking, sewing, weaving… and as they cannot survive in isolation, they create social groups to protect individuals. In all these tasks they use language. However, language is not something that replaces animal consciousness and knowledge, but emerges out of it and enormously enriches it. So what is knowledge? Here I don't think the best place to start is the philosopher's abstract enquiry. Better to begin not by asking about knowledge *of* something or other, but about knowledge *how to* do something.

A good carpenter knows *how to* saw wood straight, put up shelves that don't collapse, fit a door so that it is not proud –

and makes it all look so simple, whereas an inexperienced, butter-fingered person like me can be left cursing all morning. If you know the salsa it means you know *how to* dance the salsa. It is probably impossible to learn it from a book without hearing the music or seeing anyone dance it. We used to dance a lot in the 1960s to music like *Yellow Submarine* but when not long ago a daughter tried to teach me the salsa, I couldn't get it. In one sense I 'knew' what the salsa was, as I saw other people dancing it, but I did not know *how to* do it. My body couldn't get it; perhaps it was just not 'my' rhythm or I was past it.

The London taxi driver has to pass a fiendishly difficult exam called *The Knowledge*. This is a practical test of knowing how to find your way round all the streets of London. My father (a keen amateur jockey) once rode two winners on one day at Wincanton, his own horse Fitz Fritz, and Dorothy belonging to a neighbour. It helped that he knew the steeplechase course – that is, he knew how to ride round it and what to look out for. A farmer who 'knows his pigs' knows how to look after them so that they thrive. That practical knowledge is the basis but of course there is a lot more to get to know about pigs (as there is about London). When I was a child we had some delightful, intelligent Gloucester Old Spots and they had lots of 'character' we got to know. Likewise – though much more deeply – a new mother learns to know her baby.

A baby usually learns how to crawl before he learns the word 'crawl' and how to walk before he learns the word 'walk'. A cat can't talk at all but it can learn some things. Not so long ago I acquired a new kitten and when it was a few months old I began teaching it how to use the cat flap. In order to get into the garden it has to open the kitchen door (left ajar) with its paw, go through a cat flap at the top of the stairs, go downstairs and out through another cat flap. It has now learnt how to do this and never makes a mess in the house. Similarly, young children have to learn how to use the lavatory. But no cat can compete with Luther who, the story goes, was on the lavatory when he had his eureka moment: 'The just shall live by faith!' All the instincts humans share with animals are enriched by language and sometimes by laughter. Lovers have private jokes.

Although we learn how to do certain things in a similar way to other animals, our learning is much richer because we are speaking animals. Of their nature, languages are not private, just as human beings are not isolated 'headcases' but social animals, members of a species. Even before it can speak the baby is entering a language community and learning to talk, so although he will probably walk before he can say the word 'walk', he will still appreciate the encouraging words and cries of his doting family and gradually connect doing and saying. Similarly, a whole web and history of ideas surround dancing, carpentry and pig husbandry.

That is not to say that any of this knowledge is static or perfect. A musician might strive all her life to play better, a carpenter to increase his skills or a cabbie to learn better short cuts or new one-way systems. Knowledge *how to* starts by being *good enough* knowledge to do the job and after that, at least in some fields, you can go on learning all your life. Knowledge *how to* becomes art.

By making language, or rather, languages, humans ex-ponentially increased their powers of interacting and dealing with the Earth and each other. And with their powers, their desires for a richer life also increased. In personal life each human individual meets love, beauty, joy. As well as having to secure food and shelter, he or she has to face pain, death, boredom, loneliness or a sense of futility when they occur. Though we are not the only animals who suffer, the increased consciousness that comes with language brings both that possibility of a richer life and is a richer source of suffering.

The rest of this chapter will look at how humans use *art* to express and deal with their predicament. It will concentrate on poetry and its sister art theology (assuming that all gods are created by the human 'poetic genius'). However much our consciousness increases, knowledge that is 'sweet reason', art that speaks to our condition, must involve an acknowledgment of, and acquired familiarity with, the physicality of ourselves and the Earth. That is what we have to work with, which no art can ignore. There is a continuum. It is not the sort of continuum that when we reach 'stage 2' we have 'moved on' from 'stage 1'. We carry it all with us. We remain mortal bodies even when playing or hearing the most 'heavenly' music or enjoying the most 'divine' visions. We are speaking animals with an expanding consciousness, not spiritual beings striving to 'rise above' our animal nature. Gnosis that denies what we are is false, art that is not rooted in Earth fails, just as a building that ignores the laws of physics will fall down. Human language and art must have some recognisable relation to the world we live in, so that our word remains *incarnate,* our wisdom *embodied.*

Poetic Paradoxical Animal

Not long ago I gave a talk to the Ethical Society in the Conway Hall and when they asked me for a title I chose *The Necessity of Poetry.* I wondered whether some people's reaction to it might be: 'Don't be daft! How can poetry be necessary?' I noticed that the advertised title for my talk had in fact been changed to *The Power of Poetry,* so perhaps the organisers did think the title *The Necessity of Poetry* was just too oxymoronic.

For, what has poetry got to do with the real business of living? Some people may think that not only is poetry unnecessary but that it is a bit of an embarrassment, a bit of a nuisance, something forced upon us at school, which we can mercifully leave behind us. But I still want to argue that poetry is not only powerful but necessary.

So what is poetry? Before we look at what makes a written poem, let's consider the idea of poetry in general. If we see a swimmer diving from a high board with accomplished grace or a rider galloping a horse over a fence, we may say: 'That's poetry in motion.' Or when any skill or talent is exercised superbly: you can make a garden or bake a cake that is 'pure poetry'. If we see a mass of crocuses or daffodils in spring – 'daffodils/ that come before the swallow dares, and take/ the winds of March with beauty' – that's poetry! Or a place with a special atmosphere, a little oak wood with a stream running through it, we might call a poetic place. Or an evening walk when you are in love, or when your infant first smiles at you. Art and skill, beauty and grace, particular moments, places, encounters that 'shine' for us, that mean a lot, that's poetry. Poetry is the oomph of human life. Only the Gradgrinds of this world would say that poetry in that sense is unnecessary.

But what about poems themselves? Poems are made of language. A cat may have a favourite spot where it lies in the sun, but I don't think a cat says to itself: 'This is a poetic place.' It certainly doesn't make a poem about it. Like the cat, we are physical beings born onto Planet Earth, which is where we live the only life we have. We too are animals, but speaking animals. The power of language enables us enormously to enrich our consciousness through *conversation* and *imagination*. Using the term 'poetry' in a broad sense, I will argue that poetry is the language capable of expressing the whole breadth of our human experience, giving it its most adequate expression. Using the ordinary human power of knowing how to speak a language, poets develop it to the point where it becomes art and the utterance they produce is a poem. Poems are not necessarily about subjects that we normally regard as poetic. In fact, they can be about anything – life on Earth, maybe the whole cosmos. In this chapter I will look at what poetry is and what poetry does. Of course, in this brief space I can't possibly cover the whole breadth of human experience, just give a few tasters.

The Scope of Poetry

Praise

One of poetry's important functions is to *praise*. 'Praise. That's it!' says Rilke in his *Orpheus Sonnets*. Long ago *the* function of a court bard may have been to praise the chief – perhaps regarded as a divine figure – to praise the heroes of the tribe and their epic deeds. But now poets praise life in a far broader range of its manifestations. The original meaning of the English word 'believe', related to German *lieben,* is to cherish or hold dear. When poets praise something, they hold it dear, they give their heart to it. The Earth is so full of beauty, plants and animals, people, there are so many things to praise. First there is that lift of the heart, which the poem must then communicate in a way that lifts the hearer's or reader's heart too.

I can only give a couple of examples and I will start with one of my favourite poems about spring. This one is by Hopkins:

Nothing is so beautiful as spring –
When weeds, in wheels, shoot long and lovely and lush;
Thrush's eggs look little low heavens, and thrush

Through the echoing timber does so rinse and wring
The ear, it strikes like lightnings to hear him sing;
The glassy peartree leaves and blooms, they brush
The descending blue; that blue is all in a rush
With richness; the racing lambs too have fair their fling.

Thrush's eggs are the most beautiful blue, sometimes speckled like the birds themselves and here they are 'little low heavens'. The actual word 'blue' does not come until after we have both *seen* the eggs and *heard* the thrush's song, that 'rinses' and 'wrings' our ear so that it 'strikes like lightnings'. Then we have the 'descending blue' of the spring sky, 'brushed' by the peartree leaves and blooms – so now our sense of touch is also involved. There is a lovely, huge old peartree in St John's Garden in Regent's Park and every spring I make a point of going to sit by it. When I see the blossoms 'brushing' the sky, I remember this poem. Then we have *movement* too, as the blue is 'all in a rush' and the lambs 'race' with such gusto.

Now here is a rather different – modern – poem praising the warmth of spring but with a little jolt at the end: a short poem called 'Longed-for Warmth'.[9] Here it is complete:

How welcome this March sun is
warming my winter body.

The wind has dropped. I lizard
on a wooden bench where lake laps,
water birds glide at ease
and quack a bit, background
noise detracting nothing from a
bonus, peaceful, lazing afternoon.

Only the quick nip
of a less simple neediness.

---

[9] By DL, unpublished.

15

The poet basks in the March sunshine like a lizard and the ducks on the lake. But at the end of the poem she finds that the new sun's warmth, which she is enjoying like the other animals, is not the only warmth she yearns for.

Poetry and Science

Another sort of knowing *how to* is knowing how to distinguish, how to tell edible blackberry from poisonous belladonna, how to tell wheat from barley (barley has a beard). That is also practical knowledge. If you mistake belladonna for blackberries and gorge yourself, you could die. Language enables us to *name* these plants and pass on our knowledge to others. Language has to engage with the world as it is. Telling someone blackberries are poisonous and belladonna is good to eat is dangerous, since the opposite is the case.

As an intelligent species, we try to increase our knowledge of our own bodies, our planet and cosmos through science. Science increases our power to negotiate our lives on Earth, for example by discovering the virus that causes a deadly disease and trying to combat it. Our struggle to survive and make our lives less nasty, brutish and short requires us constantly to engage with the material world as it *really* is – not simply as we imagine it – in all the areas of our lives, through a whole range of science and technology as well as medicine, and through acquired practical skills. One way of trying to do this is by scientific research, and though the latest accepted scientific facts can always be challenged and scientists need imagination to formulate hypotheses in the first place, scientists investigate the material world and try to discover, establish how things *are* and *work*.

How grateful we are that this is the case when we are in hospital. The other day I was in Moorfields Eye Hospital and the consultant looked in my eye and explained to me what the lens is and how it can cloud over. A thousand metaphors and memories thronged through my brain, but how relieved I was that *his* interest was to look in my eye at its lens, establish exactly what state it was in, for the purpose of maintaining my sight. How I admired his expertise, dedication and skill!

Poetry may be about anything in human experience. That includes science. But poetry is *not* science. The Nicaraguan poet Ernesto Cardenal often uses scientific data in his work. His five-hundred-plus page poem called *Cosmic Canticle* is, among other things, a sort of history of the universe beginning with the Big Bang. It is also a praise poem. Here is a short extract from a section of it called *The Music of the Spheres*.[10]

> How lovely the Earth is seen from the air
> especially where it meets water!
> Animals and plants, we all
> have the same microscopic ancestor.
> We are notes in the same music.
> A universe harmonious as a harp –
> wings, neck, tail
> all keeping time –
> heart and aorta have rhythm
> like a musical instrument.

The scientific fact that 'animals and plants, we all have the same microscopic ancestor' adds greatly to the sweep and strength of this passage. But since poetry is not science, here the poet is not merely stating the scientific fact but contemplating what it means.

---

[10] Ernesto Cardenal, *The Music of the Spheres*, translated by Dinah Livingstone (Katabasis, London 1990), p. 29.

Poets may use metaphors from scientific data but they also use metaphors from the world we see around us that we know perfectly well are *not* scientific data. For example, there are many poems about sunrise or sunset. Poets writing in the past may have thought the sun really did rise in the sky and set. We now know that it is the Earth that moves in relation to the sun, but not only can we still be moved by past poems about sunrise and sunset but we may even still *write* poems about a sunrise or sunset, without in the least wanting to deny the scientific reality, because we *experience* the sun as rising or setting and it may create a certain mood in us and so on.

Warning

If an important function of poetry is to praise, another is its opposite: to speak out and protest against things that are not praiseworthy. Here is part of Blake's poem 'Holy Thursday' about child poverty:

> Is this a holy thing to see
> In a rich and fruitful land,
> Babes reduced to misery,
> Fed with cold and usurous hand?
>
> Is that trembling cry a song?
> Can it be a song of joy?
> And so many children poor?
> It is a land of poverty.

The language is very plain and works by pointing out plain contradictions. A rich country like England, with 'so many children poor', is 'a land of poverty'. And we know there is still plenty of child poverty in England to this day. The poem is called 'Holy Thursday' but 'babes reduced to misery' is an unholy state of affairs.

Or here is the beginning of Wilfred Owen's 'Anthem for Doomed Youth' denouncing the carnage of the First World War:

What passing-bells for these who die as cattle
Only the monstrous anger of the guns.
Only the stuttering rifles' rapid rattle
Can patter out their hasty orisons.
No mockeries now for them; no prayers nor bells;
Nor any voice of mourning save the choirs,
The shrill, demented choirs of wailing shells;
And bugles calling for them from sad shires.

Or here is the end of a more recent poem by Anne Beresford about turning a blind eye when something terrible is done. It is called 'Always in Another Country':[11]

Or begin in a street
and a truck passes with people standing
staring in front of them.
Where are they going?
No one asks the question
no one dares answer.

Meanwhile trees are in bloom,
the glass swept from the floor,
no truck in sight.
Think no further.

Just start again,
enter the cafe and order coffee.
When are you going to stop crying?

---

[11] Anne Beresford, *Hearing Things* (Katabasis, 2002), p. 11.

Poetry and Ethics

The passionate moral indignation in the three 'warning' poems quoted above are, of course, related to ethics. The poet wants us to see and feel that something is wrong.

However, we may also warm to passionate poetry defending a cause, which, upon reflection, we find is not so obviously good. A famous example is King Henry V's battle speech:[12]

> This day is called the feast of Crispian:
> He that outlives this day and comes safe home,
> Will stand a tip-toe when this day is named,
> And rouse him at the name of Crispian.
> He that shall live this day, and see old age,
> Will yearly on the vigil feast his neighbours
> And say, 'Tomorrow is St Crispian.'
> Then will he strip his sleeve and show his scars,
> And say, 'These wounds I had on Crispin's day.'
> Old men forget; yet all shall be forgot,
> But he'll remember with advantages
> What feats he did that day. Then shall our names,
> Familiar in his mouth as household words,
> Harry the king, Bedford and Exeter,
> Warwick and Talbot, Salisbury and Gloucester,
> Be in their flowing cups freshly remember'd.
> This story shall the good man teach his son;
> And Crispin Crispian shall ne'er go by,
> From this day to the ending of the world,
> But we in it shall be remembered.

This is tremendous stuff and has echoed down the ages of English history. Churchill obviously knew it well. However, I read that at her trial, when Joan of Arc's English judges asked

---

[12] Shakespeare, *Henry V*, IV: 3.

her: 'Are you saying that God does not love the English?' she replied: 'God does not love the English *in France*' (which proved to them that she obviously *was* a witch!). Today a reasonable English person might reflect that Joan had a point.

So although a poem's passionate plea may move us to generous sympathy and fellow feeling, thus becoming part of our moral education, we need to distinguish between poetic power and ethics. It is one task of ethics to sift our poetic treasury and *assess* it on humanist criteria. For example, in an epic poem praising the valour and noble deeds of a hero, we may admire his bravery but as he galumphs about slaying people right and left, we may conclude he is also rather a brute and not an example to follow in the ethical life.

Poetry can remind us how beautiful the Earth is and mortal beauty, says Hopkins, 'keeps warm men's wits to the things that *are,* what good means' – and therefore does *not* mean. Or as Stevie Smith says in her poem 'The Singing Cat': 'All the people warm themselves/ in the love his beauty bringeth.' But beauty and this 'warming our wits' does not *guarantee* that what we warm to is morally good.

On the other hand, we also find a lot of bad poetry with impeccable moral credentials. If we read the *in memoriam* verses published in local papers, they often have no poetic merit but may speak of a deep love for a husband, mother or grandmother that is obviously genuine. Or nowadays, we quite often find very worthy 'green' poems, whose language is intensely banal – paradoxically they lament the loss of the Earth's freshness in language that is the opposite of fresh. Nevertheless, their green agenda is of undeniable moral importance.

Poetry may include a lot of accumulated wisdom and stories that help us consider how to live. But poetry is not ethics. As Keats says, we hate poetry that has a palpable design on us, for example the eighteenth-century moralist Isaac Watts' poem that begins:

How doth the little busy bee
improve each shining hour

and goes on to lecture us to do the same.

This whole area of poetry and ethics is a very complex one. There is no room to say more about it here but it is a wide and fertile field both for the literary critic and for the moral philosopher.

The Whole Breadth of Experience

Poems don't just praise or warn. The subject matter of poetry is the whole breadth of human experience. A poem may say how things are – all kinds of things – and also how they feel and what they mean to us. Here is part of a poem by Adele David called 'Somebody's Got to Make the Meals'.[13] Martha is speaking and the poem is a comment on Velásquez' painting of *Christ in the House of Martha and Mary*. Martha says:

My hands get red and chapped
from being wet. They burn
with chilli, and smell of garlic.
That's fine by me.
The others don't want to know
what I like – the grain of the table
feeling good on my fingers;
the gutted fish all smelty cream,

---

13   In Adele David, *The Moon's Song* (Katabasis 2001), p. 9.

glittery in the bowl;
or the weight of hard boiled eggs,
how they shine, and the special roll
they make on the plate.
We're so everyday
we don't get noticed.

We apprehend the world through our five senses and this poem appeals to several senses at once. She *feels* her hands 'get red and chapped' and they *smell* of garlic. She *touches* the grain of the wood and the smooth hard-boiled eggs, she *sees* the glittery fish. This is life, she is saying, 'so everyday we don't get noticed' but also *what I like*. In his spring poem Hopkins not only appeals to our hearing with the thrush's song, but also to our sight with the blue of the eggs and the sky, and to our sense of touch, as the peartree blooms brush it. For in fact, our actual experience is 'synaesthetic': we use all our senses at once.

Poetry deals in particularities, very concrete things. For example, John Heath-Stubbs' poem 'Plato and the Waters of the Flood'[14] begins with Noah's Ark landing:

When on Armenian Ararat
or Parnassus' ridge
scrunched the overloaded keel,
pelican, ostrich,
toad, rabbit and pangolin –
all the beasts of the field –
scrambled out to possess once more
their cleansed and desolate world...

The poem is much more graphic because he names 'pelican, ostrich, toad, rabbit and pangolin' than if he had just said 'animals'. The verbs 'scrunched' and 'scrambled' are more

---

[14] John-Heath-Stubbs, *Collected Poems* (Carcanet, Manchester 1988), p. 366.

particular and vivid than if he had just said the ark 'landed' or the animals 'went out' and we enjoy the resonance of the proper names 'Armenian Ararat or Parnassus' ridge'. In the Hopkins poem 'Spring' they are not just any eggs but *thrush's eggs*, not just any tree but a *peartree* (with its particularly glorious blossom); or in the Martha poem we are not just shown a woman getting the dinner but her hands 'burn with chilli, and smell of garlic'. And she is a particular woman with a dinner guest and a sister getting on her nerves.

However, I don't agree with the dictum of a certain school of poetry: 'no ideas but in things'. Although poetry deals in the sensual and particular, it has always also dealt in ideas, the wholeness of experience, intellectual as well as sensual. 'For a tear is an intellectual thing.' In a poem the particular often has most universal resonance, embodying the abstract idea. Both the Martha poem and 'Longed-for Warmth', quoted on page 15, conclude with an idea, led up to by the preceding particularities. The last two lines of the Martha poem: 'We're so everyday/ we don't get noticed,' celebrate ordinary life and sometimes despised 'women's work'. They actually contradict Jesus' words that Mary, who has been sitting at his feet listening to him while her sister Martha slaves away in the kitchen, has 'chosen the better part'. Or in the last words of 'Longed-for Warmth', 'the quick nip/ of a less simple neediness': the poet is like the other animals enjoying the spring warmth but also *unlike* them, because in her case the 'quick nip' is a distinctly human need.

As well as everyday things perceived by our senses, our lives have dreams, maybe daydreams, also nightmares. At the beginning of his unfinished poem *The Fall of Hyperion* Keats says:

For Poesy alone can tell her dreams,
With the fine spell of words alone can save
Imagination from the sable charm
and dumb enchantment. Who alive can say,
'Thou art no Poet – mayst not tell thy dreams'?
Since every man whose soul is not a clod
Hath visions and would speak, if he had loved,
And been well nurtured in his mother tongue.

Keats says we all have dreams, visions and would tell them if we could. Poetry weaving its 'fine spell of words' enables us to tell our dreams and be released from dumbness. As well as dreams and visions, poetry *articulates* half-conscious, or even unconscious, pre-verbal feelings, desires and fears, 'the general mess of imprecision of feeling,/ Undisciplined squads of emotion', as T.S. Eliot puts it in his *Burnt Norton*. Poetry, he says, is a 'raid on the inarticulate', often involving an 'intolerable wrestle with words and meanings'. When poetry *harnesses* these strong psychic forces, these *drives,* it gains great power. Sometimes a poem may be weak and fail to move us because it is just a clever 'head' poem; it only allows in the 'daylight' and excludes the 'night' with its dark terrors and yearnings. The whole breadth of experience includes both light and darkness.

Poetry is interested in *my* life and in *other people's* lives, in everything. It is interested in seed fluff that 'floats from the willow herb/ wafts on a hot afternoon' – the seed fluff itself and the warmth of that summer afternoon. It is interested in the heady smell of an 'abundant honeysuckle wall', which becomes a 'yearning perfume of human intimacy'. Poetry can also engage with what Wordsworth calls 'those obstinate questionings/ Of sense and outward things,/ Fallings from us, vanishings...' For in our human lives what is most 'everyday' – getting the bus to work, cooking the dinner, what is most rational: paying our gas bill so that we *can* cook the dinner, packing a passport if we are going abroad – is all mixed up with feelings and meanings.

The *scope* or *content* of poetry, that is to say what the poem is *about*, is the whole breadth of human experience. At the same time a poem's *language, technique* and *form* also draw on the whole breadth of human experience. As we have seen briefly in the above examples, poetry appeals to all five senses, it is concerned first and foremost with the particular, as well as with ideas. It *embodies* and *earths* ideas, feelings and meanings, in accordance with our own nature as poetic animals. It does this in a way that makes it impossible to separate the *content* from the *form* of a poem. The medium is the message. Or, to put it another way, if you say, for example, that Keats' 'Eve of St Agnes' is about two lovers meeting and eloping, you are correct, but that is a very thin description indeed of what the poem is saying. The poem is saying a lot more because its language is very *concentrated*. We go on now to look more closely at that concentration.

Poetic Concentration

The German word for writing poetry is *dichten*, which is like the word *dicht*, meaning 'thick', closely woven like a thick hedge, though in fact, the two words are not etymologically related. In German a poet is a *Dichter*. So if we keep that serendipitous association with *dicht*, meaning thick, we can think of poetry as 'thickening' language and therefore consciousness, making it more concentrated and intense. It is the opposite of analytical language where everything is laid out, one thing after the other. Poetry is concerned with the whole of life, not just the bits or moments of it that we normally regard as 'poetic'. It is concerned with life as we live it as speaking animals in a very complex way, because as Stevie Smith puts it: 'we are so mixed'. A poem concentrates its language *both* by appealing to the senses – maybe several senses at once, as we saw in the examples given above – *and* by its ideas. It packs a lot of psychic energy into a little space. It is not 'tired' language but gives a sense of springing freshness, 'of a newly created rose', as Lorca put it. At the same time there is a sense of rightness, even inevitability: these words in this order is how the poem 'had to be'. Keats had fears that he might cease to be before his pen had 'gleaned my teeming brain'. A poem tightly packs the output of a 'teeming brain' into a shapely order.

Before we go on to look at the way in which poetry 'thickens' language and consciousness, it is worth saying a word about that mistaken etymological connection between *dichten* (= to write poetry) and *dicht* (= thick). The story goes that the poet Basil Bunting, visiting Ezra Pound in Italy, looked up the word *dichten* in a German–Italian dictionary and found *dichten* = *condensare* – the lexicographer having assumed that it was related to *dicht*, whereas in fact, disappointingly, *dichten* descends from Latin *dictare* meaning 'dictate'. That was a natural mistake to make because German, like English, commonly forms verbs from adjectives by adding –en. For example, in English we have dark, darken; light, lighten; black, blacken; red, redden; and of course thick, thicken.

The mistaken etymological link between *dicht* and *dichten* was then taken up by Pound in his *ABC of Reading* and became widely believed, even by educated Germans. It is a mistake but we can call it a lucky one; the poet and German translator Michael Hamburger regards the connection of *dichten* with *dicht* as *ben trovato* – a nice thought – for the language of poetry is indeed very condensed.

It has contributed to much fruitful thinking about poetry. For example, when the Nicaraguan poet Ernesto Cardenal (an admirer of Pound's poetry) became Sandinista Minister of Culture after the triumph of the Revolution in 1979, he wrote some *Guidelines for Writing Poetry* for the poetry workshops that were set up all over the country. One *Guideline* was: 'Try to condense the language as much as possible… A poem may be very long but each of its lines should be in very condensed language.' Other guidelines included the advice that 'poetry needs to be based on things which reach us through our senses' – things which can be touched, tasted, heard, seen and smelt – and to prefer concrete terms to vaguer ones, for 'good poetry is usually made out of very concrete things'. He recommended the use of particular, rather than more general terms (to give some English examples: say 'willow' rather than just 'tree' or 'celandine' rather than just 'flower') and the use of proper names.[15]

Now we go on to consider some of the other main ways in which poetic concentration is increased.

Sound and Rhythm

A poem is 'thickened' not only by its concentrated content but also by the physical qualities of the actual words it uses. Poetry is not only our 'highest' language but also the most embodied. As *incarnate* word, it beautifully suits the expression of our own being as poetic *animals*. Just as we remain mortal bodies even when enjoying the most spiritual experiences, our highest poetry makes the fullest use of the physical resources of spoken language. Words are the poet's *material*. Words are physically produced by human lungs, throats, tongues, lips and

---

[15] Excellent examples of the telling use of proper names in poetry can be found in Shakespeare's Henry V's speech, quoted on page 20 ('then shall our names,/ Familiar in his mouth as household words, /Harry the king, Bedford and Exeter…'); and in the extract from Blake's *Jerusalem*, quoted on page 104.

teeth. Indeed, languages are called 'tongues'. Hopkins called poetry 'the darling child of speech and lips'. Rhythm, together with the phonic quality and pattern of sounds in words, can give enormous, even ecstatic, pleasure.

The *sounds* of words are very important in poetry, for example whether the vowels used are 'dark' and formed at the back of the mouth or lighter front vowels. English is fortunate that its word 'dark' has the most open back vowel ɑː – that is why the doctor tells you to say *aaah!* How we hear that darkness in Milton's Samson's tremendous protest against his blindness:

> O dark, dark, dark, amid the blaze of noon,
> irrecoverably dark, total eclipse
> without all hope of day!

In contrast, the words 'blaze' and 'day' have a close front diphthong, here recalling the *absent* light.

A series of words using vowels formed at the back of the mouth can have a dark, heavy effect: For example: *'Haw! haw! haw!' laughed the hard strong father.* Contrast that with a string of front vowels, which sound much lighter in both senses: *Drip drip drip pitter patter rain.*

Onomatopoeia is a playful way of suiting the sounds of words to their meaning. John Heath-Stubbs' poem *Christus Natus Est*[16] uses the legend that the animals speak on Christmas night. His animals speak Latin, which here pleasingly mimics each animal's proper noise. The cock crows: *'Christus natus est'* – Christ is born – which has the same rhythm as cock-a-doodle-doo. The duck quacks: *'Quando?'* –

---

[16] *Collected Poems,* p. 67.

When? The raven croaks: *'In hac nocte'* – tonight. The ox lows: *'Ubi?'* – Where? The lamb bleats the reply: *'Bethlehem!'*

The *pattern* of sounds also matters, what sounds are repeated in a pleasing order. So does the *rhythm* of stressed and unstressed beats, which we respond to as physical beings with beating hearts. Poetry is language to which people may have a strong physical response – making the heart beat faster or the hair rise on the back of your neck.

The earliest English poetry had a four-stress line and its other main technique was *alliteration*, that is, three out of the four stressed words had the same initial consonant (or consonant beginning a word's first stressed syllable). Here is an example from the medieval *Piers Plowman*,[17] because earlier poems written in Old English, such as *Beowulf,* are difficult now for us to understand without a dictionary. Piers sees a great looming prison and asks a lady what it is.

> That *dungeon* in the *dale* that *dreadful* is of sighte
> What *may* it be*mean, Madam,* I you beseeche?

The lady answers:

> That is the *castle* of *care* – whoso *cometh* therein
> may *ban*[18] that he *born* was to *body* or to soul.

The alliteration and the four-beat line give vigour to the question and to the answer. Alliteration is still used today and has been used throughout the poetic history of English, not necessarily in such a strictly formal pattern. For example, we quoted a line above from Perdita's list of spring flowers in Shakespeare's *Winter's Tale*: 'daffodils/ that come before the

---

[17] William Langland, *The Vision of Piers Plowman,* Passus I, lines 59–62.
[18] At the time of writing 'ban' meant 'curse'.

swallow dares'. How much stronger that line is than if she had said 'daffodils/ that come before the swallow arrives' or even 'narcissus that come before the swallow dares'. The alliteration helps to give the daffs a thrusting life. Or in Hopkins' 'Spring' poem, alliteration conveys a sense of surging energy in: 'that blue is all in a *rush*/ With *richness*; the *racing* lambs…'

As English poetry developed, other rhythms or metres were used. In their verse dramas the great Elizabethan poets mainly used a longer line, the iambic pentameter with five beats:

Was this the face that launched a thousand ships
And burnt the topless towers of Ilium?[19]

Old English poetry was not usually rhymed but gradually rhyme and formal rhyme schemes were introduced as another means of concentrating the language. Look again at the Hopkins sonnet quoted on pages 14–15 – just the first eight lines of the sonnet, called the octet – and we find there are only two rhymes in it: *lush/thrush/brush/rush* and *spring/wring/sing/fling*. Hopkins has used them very skilfully; they are not too obtrusive and readers may not even realise there are only two rhymes the first time the poem is heard. At the same time the rhymes bind the octet together and the soft sound of *lush/ brush/rush*, together with the lighter ting-a-ling sound of *spring/sing/fling*, provide its two keynotes. Nowadays poets wanting to refresh the language use formal rhyme schemes less often but they do still use rhymes, sometimes with great skill.

---

[19]   Christopher Marlowe, *Dr Faustus* V: 1.

Allusion

Befitting us as a speaking animal species, poems (and ideas) are not isolated. Another way in which a poem thickens language and consciousness, increasing 'connectivity', is by being a conversation in a tradition, by allusions. This can be done in a rather heavy-handed way or with the light touch of 'answer, echo, answer'. The problem is, the lighter the touch, the finer your audience's ear must be.

No language is private; it belongs to a linguistic community which probably has a long history. A new poem takes part in a conversation in a tradition, sometimes implicitly and sometimes more overtly. Here are some lines from another 'warning' poem, called 'The Excluded'.[20] Standing on London Bridge on a dreary day, the poet looks down at the grey river and 'enters the crying', hearing 'the keen agony of the lonely,/ the roaring of the ignored,/ the fury of the defeated,/ the tortured screaming an ultimate No.' The poem continues:

Thousand upon thousand
of the excluded crowded in,
rank on rank of sorrow.
I had not thought there would be so many
uttering that intolerable sound.

When 'thousand upon thousand/ of the excluded crowded in', the poem says: 'I had not thought there would be so many/ uttering that intolerable sound.' That is a direct allusion to T.S. Eliot's poem *The Waste Land*, in which:

A crowd flowed over London Bridge, so many,
I had not thought death had undone so many.

---

[20] In DL, *May Day* (Katabasis 1997), p. 50.

Eliot in his turn is alluding to Dante's *Inferno*. When Dante visits the underworld he is amazed at the crowds: *'ch'io non averei creduto/ che morte tanta n'avesse disfatta:* 'I would not have believed death had undone so many.' These are all people excluded from Paradise. 'Rank on rank' is an echo of the First-World-War memorial hymn, 'O Valiant Hearts', but here the 'thousand upon thousand' are not those who 'to your glory came':[21] they are excluded. They are 'uttering that intolerable sound', and the poem goes on to say 'that ultrasonic pitch had greater power/ than any laser to shatter the city,/ with all its gates and bridges, however magnificent and strong.' So here it is 'thickened' again by an allusion to the nursery rhyme 'London Bridge is Falling Down'.

Incidentally, as poets are writing within a cultural tradition, sometimes they use allusions without being conscious of doing so at the time of writing and only twig later, when they re-visit their own poem or someone else points it out to them. Here is an example. At the end of a poem about my small grandson I describe him coming back from a foray into muddy grass:

> Back on the tarmac he lumbers
> with hunched shoulders: 'Rrrr!
> I'm a monster!' emerging from primal slime
> into imagination and language,
> shambling the long human road.
> The buds on the trees are still shut fast
> but today seem to promise
> something will happen soon,
> and from that high branch, voice
> like a silver lancet, the robin singing
> pierces the soul, the hope,
> the pain, the beauty of it. [22]

---

[21] In fact, this is the 'glory' Wilfred Owen attacked in his 'Anthem for Doomed Youth', quoted on page 19.

[22] DL, 'At the Start' published in *Acumen* 66, January 2010.

I know I did not realise at the time that the 'silver lancet' of the robin singing piercing the soul was an allusion to Jesus' presentation in the temple in Luke's Gospel. About her son the old man Simeon tells Mary: 'And a sword will pierce your own soul too.'[23] As well as referring to Mary's own future, by analogy this story can applied to the constant anxious care and pain mothers (and grandmothers) suffer all their lives for their offspring. So it was obviously somewhere at the back of my mind when I contemplated my grandson 'shambling the long human road'. (The poem was written in Darwin's centenary year and what was at the forefront of my mind was evolution.) This is just one example of how a poem may tell not just the reader but also the author things they didn't know they knew.

We are speaking animals, not isolated but members of a linguistic community, a species. Because a human being made it, once a poem has been written it belongs to us all. Poetry enriches not just the individual consciousness but our common humanity. Ways of 'thickening' consciousness used by poetry become *insights*: they pass into the fabric of the mind. For example, when we remember poems associated with a particular place, it becomes more meaningful to us. I expect, like me, most Londoners have special places in London, to which they bring personal memories, associations, stories, bits of history, snatches of poetry to enrich them.

Symbolic Language

We use language to name things and distinguish them from one another. To negotiate the real world, we need to know that a field mushroom is delicious to eat and a death cap mushroom can kill us. And in a language community we can pass that information on to others. Out for a walk, a child

---

23   Lk 2: 35.

learning to speak will point out names of things he has learnt: 'Doggy!', 'Duck!' with enormous gusto, a bit like one-word praise poems celebrating the world.

However, Coleridge seems to be right that nature gives us our 'shaping spirit of imagination' at birth. One of the most astonishing things about watching a two-year-old learn to talk is that metaphor, symbol and 'let's pretend' (as well as joking) seem to come naturally as soon as the words are acquired. The child will go into a corner and say: 'I'm a pony in a barn,' and neigh. Or: 'I'm a naughty goblin,' and run off with a biscuit. Or the child can wave a magic wand and tell his grandfather: 'You're a cat.' Grandfather is expected to miaow. The child then chooses when to wave the wand again and turn Grandfather back into himself.

The child not only learns to *pretend* but to know he is doing so. A toy car is *like* and *unlike* a real car, as the child knows when he says 'Brm brm!' and makes the toy car rev up. A stick can be a sword and he can poke his father with it saying: 'You're a dragon and you're dead!' Perhaps his father will oblige and fall down and both know it is a game. A year or so later, when the child is about four, he may enjoy Stevie Smith's poem about 'Fafnir the Dragon', which puts the dragon's point of view. He can *put himself in the dragon's place*. Children learning to talk not only enjoy sounds and rhythms but have a native gift for symbol and metaphor. A poetic potential is not something 'added on' to language but is inherent in it: we are born to be not merely speaking animals but poetic animals.

This use of symbolic language is a vital means of poetic concentration or thickening. Poems employ *simile* and *metaphor*. We can say 'my love is like a rose' (or a 'red red rose') or we can say someone is a lion, a dog, a toad etc. Sometimes some of those comparisons may seem a bit unfair to the animals! In the poem 'Longed-for Warmth' the poet sitting in the sun says: 'I lizard/ on a wooden bench'. Here the animal metaphor is a *verb* meaning 'I bask like a lizard'. At the end of the poem 'the quick nip/ of a less simple neediness' sharply jabs the poet, just as the seemingly calm ducks on the water sometimes make a sudden sharp nip. Or in the lines: 'Cloud shapes canter over the twiggy trees' the clouds are like race horses. It is a winter skyscape because the trees are 'twiggy' (like fences in steeplechase), and fast-moving, probably windy. In the Hopkins poem 'Spring' the thrush's song 'rinses' and 'wrings' the ear. The bird's wonderful song is compared to two processes used on a mundane washday – rinsing and wringing – but the result is a sense of lifted spirits.

As well as having enormous variety, everything on our Earth has a family resemblance. Part of learning to talk is learning the names of things, so that you can distinguish them, tell them apart. At the same time we see how one thing is *like* another. Here is just one small example. This poem, 'November',[24] ends:

> Flutter, flit and tweet,
> keen to survive the coming cold.
> Each little rustle,
> sudden or stray thought,
> might be a bird
> or a falling leaf.

Not only are the flitting small birds like the free-floating brown leaves, but both are like a 'sudden or stray thought'. The noises are very small: 'flutter, flit and tweet… Each little rustle'. Of course, a thought makes no noise at all but it is as if it 'rustled'. That metaphor involves sight and sound, but we can have metaphors for all the senses. For example, the smell

---

[24] In DL, *Kindness* (Katabasis 2007), p. 24.

of the Earth is 'a draught of strong ale, warm, huddled cattle', which involves smell, taste and touch. We can also have *rhythmic metaphors*. A memorable example (which young children love) is the galloping anapaestic tetrameter:

> I sprang to the stirrup, and Joris, and he.
> I galloped, Dirck galloped, we galloped all three.

In his Preface to the *Lyrical Ballads* Wordsworth speaks of 'a principle which must be well known to those who have made any of the arts the object of accurate reflection; namely the pleasure which the mind derives from the *perception of similitude in dissimilitude*. This principle is the great spring of the activity of our minds and their chief feeder.' This similitude in dissimilitude – likeness in difference and distinction in likeness – is one of the ways in which poetry expands or 'thickens' our consciousness. There is the shock of recognition that something is *like* something else and the pleasing tension that it is also *unlike*.

A metaphor compares two things in this way. For the metaphor to have poetic power, its 'vehicle' (that is, the thing to which something else is being compared) must be well rooted in the material Earth, *physically* well grounded. For example, in Hopkins' poem 'Hurrahing in the Harvest' (using a metaphor which his friend Robert Bridges tut-tutted was 'in poor taste') he compares Christ (here the *tenor* of the metaphor) to the beautiful hills of his beloved 'wild Wales' (the metaphor's *vehicle*):

> And the azurous hung hills are his world-wielding shoulder
> Majestic – as a stallion stalwart, very violet-sweet!

Hopkins had a Jesuit training in philosophy and theology and of course he did not think the blue hills were really Christ's (or the Greek god Atlas') shoulder. It is a metaphor expressing a moment of ecstasy. Its poetic power (the metaphor's substance or vehicle) derives from the fact that strong and beautiful blue hills, male shoulders and horses physically exist and can be apprehended by our senses.

We note that when a metaphor makes one thing *symbolise* something else, or a simile says one thing is *like* something else, the two things do not correspond one hundred percent. For example, if I say: 'She's like a breath of fresh air', in this simile I mean she revives us, lifts our spirits, but not that she is as invisible as air. Or when I say: 'David is a lion', in this metaphor I mean David is strong and like a lion in some respects, but I do not expect him to eat me! As Thomas Aquinas puts it:

> Hence the name 'lion' is applied first to the animal containing the whole nature of a lion, and which is properly so called, before it is applied to a man who shows something of a lion's nature, as courage, or strength, or the like; and of whom it is said by way of similitude.[25]

Another striking example of a metaphor only *partly* applying is the parable of the Good Shepherd, who 'gives his life for his sheep'. Of course, a good shepherd cares devotedly for his sheep – that part of the metaphor applies – but the shepherd's *purpose* in looking after the sheep is to rear them until they make good wool or good eating, when they will be slaughtered – that part of the metaphor does *not* apply in this parable.

Supernaturalisation

Keats called trees 'mighty senators'. He personified them. Others have called trees gods. And Hildegard of Bingen spoke of 'greenness' as divine. I often talk to trees and can quite see

---

[25] *Summa Theologica* I: 33: 3.

how people could think of particularly noble trees as gods. I also say things like 'Sun, please shine today' or 'Rain, rain, go away'. When it thunders, it is easy to imagine a mighty being or god grumbling overhead. Sometimes a god is simply a superhuman fictional character without being a god *of* anything, but commonly a god is the supernaturalisation of something on Earth or in the cosmos, who may then also acquire a rich character and biography.

As Blake put it: 'The ancient Poets animated all sensible objects with Gods or Geniuses, calling them by the names and adorning them with the properties of woods, rivers, mountains, lakes, cities, nations, and whatever their enlarged and numerous senses could perceive.' 'Animating' sensible objects with gods is a poetic activity. Personification, like metaphor, is a poetic trope, symbolic language. We could call 'supernaturalisation' another poetic trope, akin to personification. All supernatural beings were created by the 'ancient Poets': they are human creations. Then 'a system was formed' so that people ended up 'choosing forms of worship from poetic tales. And at length they pronounced that the Gods had ordered such things. Thus men forgot that All deities reside in the human breast.'

What we may describe as more 'primitive' religion thinks of the sun or rain or thunder itself as a god. Then people may go on to think of the god as the master or maker of the sun, rain and thunder. Mighty Jove has thunderbolts. It is not a long step between saying 'God thunders' and 'God makes thunder'. And it is still a form of personification. God is the supernatural force or divine person who makes thunder, or when you get to monotheism, God is the divine person who makes everything. If we read the holy books about the monotheistic God of Christianity, Judaism and Islam, we find that over the centuries this God has changed quite a bit.

Stories, either of a multitude of gods and goddesses or a single 'one true God', are *poetic tales*, many of them dating back to a pre-scientific age.

As well as being or making cosmic forces and things on Earth, gods or God can be a personification of human activities – such as love and war – and capabilities, actual or idealised. Men can be fathers and God is called an 'almighty father'. Human beings can love and they can personify God *as* love, saying God is Love. Once God is a person he or she can be a character in a story. He walks in the Garden of Eden.[26] In the rather horrific story of the sacrifice of Isaac he orders Abraham to kill his only son (but then relents).[27] In *Paradise Lost* God the Father and God the Son are both characters and the whole cosmos throngs with good and evil angels.[28]

What is the point of inventing these supernatural beings? First there is the poetic point. These personifications or supernaturalisations express our deep experiences of the world. Some things we encounter in the world give us a sense of awe, 'something far more deeply interfused', a sense of the holy. For Blake: 'Everything that lives is holy.' As we are naturally poetic animals, we try to express this in poetic terms. We said that we called things, places and encounters that 'shine' for us poetic. The Indo-European root *div*, from which its word 'god' is derived, means 'shine' and is also related to 'sky'. So a god is a 'shining one'. There is no need to seek a supernatural explanation. People who regard God as real are unaware that they are using a poetic trope, rather like Molière's *bourgeois gentilhomme*, who was amazed to discover he had been speaking prose. All stories of supernatural beings are fictional because there *are* no supernatural beings. We can enjoy them

---

[26] Gen 3: 8.
[27] Gen 22: 1–14.
[28] Milton's theology, by the way, seems to be Arian. See pages 110–11.

as stories (just as we can enjoy poems about the sun rising like a fiery chariot) and they often enshrine wisdom.

Ordinary people in England today are quite shy of poetry. Perhaps that is related to the way in which they are also shy of theology. Genesis begins with two creation stories, both of which are, of course, pre-scientific. In the second of these the main character is Yahweh, who also appears in the succeeding story about the tree of knowledge. Yahweh-God comes over as very human indeed, worried that Adam will be lonely without a companion, jealous to preserve his own knowledge and power. They are good stories but it is obviously absurd to treat them as historical or scientific. I think the religious fundamentalists who try to do this are suffering from a nervousness of *poetry*. They insist these stories must be literally, scientifically true with a plain prose meaning. They are mistaking the category or genre of these tales because they think only plain prose meaning has any value. The same could be said for atheist zealots.

Although the Earth and our material human bodies are given to, in another sense humanity is also what we make of it – it is a project or goal, what we as individuals and a species can become. Humans are ambitious and want to know not only how to survive, but how to live with meaning. They make art, and once made, this art shapes *them*. They try to make *living* an art. As poetic animals, we keep seeking a 'thicker' – expanded, intenser – consciousness and here theology comes in as a sister art to poetry, creating supernatural beings, who nevertheless all 'reside in the human breast'. That poetic quest remains even for those who have 'taken leave of God'. Not everyone likes writing or even reading poetry. But here poetry is a paradigm for every kind of knowing how to that becomes an art, every grace that is 'pure poetry'.

The way in which poetry contributes to the making of our humanity is by expanding our consciousness, increasing its *connectivity*. Poetry is an older language than science or philosophy and more all-embracing. New poetry must also constantly refresh the language. Poetry is beauty so old and so new. Using all the techniques at its disposal, poetry is the most *concentrated* language. It is the language most suited to our nature as speaking animals because the *physical* qualities of the spoken word (sound and rhythm) are more important in poetry than in any other forms of speech. Poetry deals with our whole physical experience of negotiating the world in which we find ourselves. At the same time 'poetry alone can tell our dreams': it is the language most adequate to our aspirations, which is why people often turn to it at very important moments in their lives.

In his lecture on the *Theory and Function of the Duende*,[29] which is 'a mysterious power that everyone feels but that no philosopher has explained', Lorca says: 'All the arts are capable of possessing *duende,* but naturally the field is widest in music, in dance, and in spoken poetry, because they require a living body as an interpreter – they are forms that arise and die ceaselessly, and are defined by an exact present.' The appearance of the *duende,* he says:

> gives a sensation of freshness wholly unknown, having the quality of a newly created rose, of miracle, and produces in the end an almost religious enthusiasm. In all Arabic music, dance, or song, the appearance of the *duende* is greeted with vociferous shouts of *'Alá! Alá!'*: 'God! God!' which are not far from the *olé* of bullfighting. And in the singing of Southern Spain, the presence of the *duende* is followed by shouts of *¡Viva Dios!'*

---

[29] 'Theory and Function of the *Duende*' in Lorca, *Selected Poems,* trans. J.L. Gili (Penguin 1960), pp. 131, 2.

Poets must each find their own voice to express themselves, the Earth and humanity – what it is and could be. Voice is first and foremost a human bodily power. Poetry does not 'float' or 'rise above' that human bodily power to become 'pure spirit'. On the contrary, rather than *abstracting*, it uses its bodily, sensual capabilities to the utmost. It beautifully suits the poetic paradoxical animals we are: matter 'all the way up', spirit 'all the way down'. It is most sublime when it is most embodied. As the old theological adage has it: *'Gratia non tollit naturam sed perficit:* Grace does not destroy nature but perfects it.' Poetry is incarnate word.

When we look at the scope of poetry and particularly its use of symbolic language, there is no need to suppose that the supernatural realm and supernatural beings are anything other than poetic creations. The remaining three chapters of this book will reflect on some 'poetic tales' in the Christian story, in which the Incarnate Word is central.

Chapter 2

Mother and Father

Mother

We might go for a walk with a friend on a beautiful autumn day but when that friend exclaims ecstatically how beautiful and how varied the colours of the leaves are, what a lot of berries and how rich their red, we might respond: 'I don't feel very poetic today. I've got a cold.' Or as Coleridge put it in his 'Dejection – an Ode': 'I see not feel how beautiful they are.' When beautiful things on Earth make us feel rapturous, we think of this heightened awareness as a poetic feeling. As part of that poetic feeling, as well as rapture we often have a sense of awe and wonder, as if we are in the presence of what is 'holy'.

Blake said it was the 'ancient *Poets*' who 'animated all sensible objects with Gods or Geniuses, calling them by the names and adorning them with the properties of woods, rivers, mountains, lakes, cities, nations, and whatever *their enlarged and numerous senses could perceive.*' Poetic awareness enlarges and increases the senses. This awareness apprehends the *being* of things. In his poem 'Binsey Poplars – felled 1879', Hopkins begins:

My aspens dear, whose airy cages quelled,
Quelled or quenched in leaves the leaping sun,
All felled, felled, are all felled.

Six years earlier he had written in his diary:

The ashtree growing in the corner of the garden was felled. It was lopped first: I heard the sound and looking out and seeing it maimed there came at that moment a great pang and I wished to die and not to see the inscapes of the world destroyed any more.[30]

Such poetic awareness may *personify*, for example address a tree or an animal: 'You glorious, sturdy oak…', 'O my darling pussy cat…' Although they can't talk, animals and trees are companionable. My cat Etty likes to sit beside me on the sofa in the evening. As the Dorset dialect poet William Barnes says:

However lonesome we might be
The trees would still be company.

Then with another poetic trope, akin to personification, heightened poetic awareness may *supernaturalise* that being. Trees and cats have quite often been regarded as gods. Heightened poetic awareness is not uncommon. Everyone 'whose soul is not a clod' is capable of poetic vision, some people more than others, everyone on some days more than others.

Some people today think poetry is rather naff, or something to grow out of. If you rhapsodise over some beautiful ducks swimming on a lake, these people take pleasure in remarking: 'Good eating!' It is quite difficult to speculate about the consciousness of our polytheistic ancestors. But it is quite easy to imagine *why* they 'animated' so many beings and forces in nature as spirits or gods. This is a poetic mode of apprehension, which we too can knowingly share. And presumably, our ancestors also shared some of our more prosaic modes of apprehension, and as well as, maybe,

---

[30] Gerard Manley Hopkins, *Selected Prose,* ed. Gerald Roberts (Oxford University Press 1980), p. 56.

thinking a duck was imbued with a spirit, also saw that it was 'good eating'.

As well as believing in all sorts of gods and spirits including perhaps a 'Sky Father' and/or Sun God, many ancient cultures regarded the whole Earth as a Great Goddess and often called her Mother. Goddesses and gods are poetic creations but that does not mean that the beings and forces they personify, or whose 'supernaturalisations' they are, are not real. The Earth Mother goddess is a poetic creation but the Earth is real, physical, material. We evolved from her. It is she who has made us and not we ourselves. She existed before us and will continue to exist after we are all gone. The postmodernist idea that everything is reducible to language is nonsense. It is a denial of the physical – mortal, vulnerable – *reality* of the Earth. It is a convenient partner to the aggressive capitalist *exploitation* of the Earth merely for profit, which is now endangering both the planet and our species. Just as postmodernism reduces the Earth to language, aggressive capitalism *commodifies* it, so that, in effect, it is reduced to money.

Perhaps the poetic mode of apprehending the Earth is truer. The poet's 'enlarged and numerous senses' view the Earth with reverence, and, symbolically, as spiritual, as divine. 'Everything that lives is holy.' Like God, the cosmos says: 'I AM.' Like Goddess, the Earth says: 'I AM.' Cosmos and Earth together are the supreme I AM to excite our awe and wonder. Personifying or supernaturalising them is merely a poetic mode of expressing that awe and wonder.

The cosmos can't speak, the Earth can't speak. We, who evolved out of cosmic dust through all the millions of years of Earth's evolution, are Earth's voice. We are her speech organ. We can speak for her. We can speak her. And supremely, that is the role of poetry. 'For Poesy alone can tell her dreams,/ With the fine spell of words alone can save/ Imagination from the sable charm/ and dumb enchantment.' It is the role of human language, and poetry in particular, to release the Earth from its 'dumb enchantment'. We may call the Earth a Goddess, the Great Mother, and that poetic trope of supernaturalisation corresponds to the *reality* that she produced us and we depend on her for everything. But Earth does not see herself or call *herself* a Goddess; we do. As Keats says later in *The Fall of Hyperion*:

> Whereon there grew
> A power within me of enormous ken
> To see as a God sees, and take the depth
> Of things as nimbly as the outward eye
> Can size and shape pervade.

It is human beings that have the power to 'see as a God sees' and to say what they see. That innate power is a poetic power and it will develop more in some human beings than in others. More people will develop the power to *see* than the power to *say* 'with the fine spell of words'.

It is not hard to see why our ancestors regarded the Earth as a Great Mother. They saw that she is our home, she provides us with shelter, food and drink. We could not have come into being without her and she sustains us while we live. As well as that, she is mighty, teeming with exuberant variety, and very beautiful. We who know the story of evolution, how everything belongs together in one marvellous ecosystem, have even more reason to regard the Earth with awe and reverence.

When the Earth is thought of as the Great Mother, she is central and the sky and the sun and the stars are thought of in relation to her. The English are used to being gently mocked because they talk so much about the weather. When I go through our small park in the early morning to get my newspaper, I meet gardeners and neighbours walking their dogs or going to work. We greet each other: 'Lovely morning!' or 'Gosh, it's wet!' or 'Frosty today!' These greetings are not inane. They are a kind of phatic communion expressing our common lot as Earth creatures and the feel of being here on this new day.

In the previous chapter, we said one major function of poetry was to praise. We are Earth's voice. We can praise the Earth and all its marvellous variety of landscapes and creatures living on it. We can express how it feels to be living on Earth, and how it feels at different times of day. Well-known morning hymns such as 'The morning, the bright and the beautiful morning,/ is up...' start by praising the morning and then go on to say: 'O now let us haste to our heavenly Father,/ hasten to give him the praise that is due.' There is no reason at all why we should not praise morning on Earth for its own sake and many poets have done so all over the world, from epic Homer with his 'rosy-fingered dawn' onwards.

In the poem 'Voices'[31] morning is another chance:

Then on a summer morning
I wake to the heavenly sense
of earthly energies restored,
another day, another chance.
The night is over.

And here is an Italian poem, the famous (and famously difficult to translate) two-word poem 'Morning' by Ungaretti, which gives a wonderful feeling of morning light and its vastness: *'M'illumino d'immenso.'* Literally this means 'I

---

[31]   In DL, *Presence* (Katabasis 2003), p. 13.

illuminate myself of immense,' which sounds horrible. My best translation to date is 'I am lit by the immense,' which still does not reproduce the sequence of sounds repeated in both the words, which give the original poem much of its power: m, n, o – two nasal consonants and the final 'o', which is a pure vowel in Italian, not a diphthong as in English.

The monastic canonical Hours of Matins (plus Lauds), Prime, Terce, Sext, None, Vespers and Compline (Morning, 6 a.m., 9 a.m., noon, 3 p.m. Evensong and End of Day) *hallow* each phase of the day. Such praise too can also be directed to the Earth herself and life on Earth, rather than to a 'heavenly Father'. Countless poems have done so or simply expressed the *feeling* of a certain time of day. A poem by García Lorca, written in the summer heat of Spain, begins: 'I thirst for shade, says afternoon.' As well as morning and midday, evening and twilight have inspired a great wealth of poems. Though it is often regarded as a children's poem, I still love Walter de la Mare's 'Nod':

> Softly along the road of evening,
> In a twilight dim with rose,
> Wrinkled with age and drenched with dew,
> Old Nod the shepherd goes.

> His drowsy flock streams on before him,
> Their fleeces charged with gold,
> To where the sun's last beam leans low
> On Nod the shepherd's fold.

The Hours of the day go together with a liturgical year, which celebrates the cycle of Earth's seasons, as well as a linear history of the making of humanity, still incomplete (about which more in the next chapter). Christmas, at the winter solstice, celebrates the birth of Jesus and the 'rebirth' of the sun. The Magnificat 'O Antiphon' for the actual day of the solstice, 21^{st,} December, equates Jesus with the rising sun: *'O Oriens, splendor lucis aeternae et sol justitia*: O Rising One (Daystar), splendour of eternal light, and sun of justice, come and bring light to those sitting in darkness and the shadow of death.' Easter, which celebrates Christ's resurrection, is a spring festival named after Eostre, the Anglo-Saxon Earth goddess of spring and fertility.

There are huge numbers of poems about the seasons, many without any supernatural element, that speak about Earth's turning year and the feel of living and working at different times. In chapter 1 we quoted Hopkins' 'Spring'. The chorus of Shakespeare's song: 'It was a lover and his lass' is 'In springtime, the only pretty ring time,/ when birds do sing "hey ding-a-ding-a-ding",/ sweet lovers love the spring.' At the end of Chaucer's *Parliament of Fowls*, 'my rightful lady, Goddess of Nature', also called 'the noble Goddess of Kind', pronounces judgment and all the different birds fly away with their mates in a jubilant chorus:

> And when this work all brought was to an ende,
> To every fowl Nature gave his make
> By even accord, and on their way they wende,
> And, Lord, the blisse and joye that they make!

They sing together:

> Now welcome, summer, with thy sunne softe,
> That hast this winter's weather overshake,
> And driven away the longe nightes blacke.

In Keats' *Ode to Autumn*, Autumn is personified as an Earth goddess in autumn mode:

> Who hath not seen thee oft amid thy store?
> Sometimes whoever seeks abroad may find

Thee sitting careless on a granary floor,
Thy hair soft-lifted by the winnowing wind;
Or on a half-reaped furrow sound asleep,
Drowsed with the fume of poppies, while thy hook
Spares the next swath and all its twinèd flowers…
Or by a cider-press, with patient look
Thou watchest the last oozings hours by hours.

Towards the end of William Morris' utopian novel *News from Nowhere,* when they are preparing for the harvest feast, the heroine Ellen exclaims:

O me! O me! How I love the Earth, and the seasons, and weather, and all things that deal with it, and all that grows out of it!'[32]

Human beings are Earth's voice and when it is a poetic voice it has a 'freshness', like the Earth herself. That is a quality of what Lorca called the *duende,* 'the mysterious power that everyone feels but that no philosopher has explained'. The *duende,* he adds, 'is in fact the spirit of the Earth'.[33]

In his book *Life, Life*[34] Don Cupitt contrasts 'world people' and 'life people'. 'World people,' he says disparagingly, 'see us as being set in a ready-made, ready-ordered physical world, which must be studied closely if we are to act effectively. For life people, by contrast, knowledge and the physical world are relatively unimportant. Consider how rarely Shakespeare's characters pay close attention to their physical environment.' Life people, says Cupitt, 'scarcely notice their physical environment, because they are so absorbed by the varied ways

32 *News from Nowhere* reprinted in *Three Works of William Morris* (Lawrence and Wishart, London 1986).
33 'Theory and Function of the *Duende*', p. 127.
34 Don Cupitt, *Life, Life* (Polebridge Press, Santa Rosa USA, 2003), pp. 10–11.

in which people interact with each other… Life people are non-realists. They are not interested in the idea of an intelligible, real, non-human "it" world.' Don Cupitt does not mention any particular play and his blanket claim that Shakespeare's characters 'scarcely notice their physical environment' is not true. To give just a couple of examples, starting with King Lear in the storm:[35]

> Blow, winds, and crack your cheeks! rage! blow!
> You cataracts, and hurricanoes spout,
> Till you have drenched our steeples, drowned the cocks!
> You sulphurous and thought-executing fires,
> Vaunt-couriers of oak-cleaving thunderbolts
> Singe my white head.

Lear goes on to say the storm is not as unkind as his daughters have been. He is reluctant to be led indoors because 'this tempest will not give me leave to ponder on things would hurt me more'. The storm is the central image and the dark heart of the play.

The Forest itself is one of the main themes of *As You Like It*. In contrast to the violent hatreds of the Court in Act I, Act II opens with the banished Duke enthusing at length about life in the Forest, which Amiens praises in his song:[36]

> Under the greenwood tree,
> Who loves to lie with me,
> And turn his merry note
> Unto the sweet bird's throat,
> Come hither, come hither, come hither.
> Here shall he see
> No enemy
> But winter and rough weather.

---

[35] III: 2.
[36] II: 5.

The characters continually talk about the Forest, often contrasting it with the Court. The shepherd Corin argues with Touchstone:[37]

> Those that are good manners at the court are as ridiculous in the country as the behaviour of the country is most mockable at the court. You told me you salute not at the court but you kiss your hands: that courtesy would be uncleanly if courtiers were shepherds.

'Instance,' demands Touchstone. Corin replies: 'Why, we are still handling our ewes and their fells, you know, are greasy.'

Just one more example. In *The Winter's Tale*[38] Perdita and the disguised King Polixines discuss grafting, which she disapproves of and he, ironically in the circumstances, recommends. She describes what grows at every season in her garden and would offer them to her guests according to their age. Among the spring flowers she would like to give her love Florizel are:

> daffodils
> That come before the swallow dares, and take
> The winds of March with beauty; violets dim,
> But sweeter than the lids of Juno's eyes
> Or Cytherea's breath; pale primroses
> That die unmarried, ere they can behold
> Bright Phoebus in his strength, a malady
> Most incident to maids; bold oxlips and
> The crown imperial...

All these are cottage garden flowers that bloom between March and May and she offers them to him because it is the

---

[37] III: 2.
[38] IV: 3.

springtime of her love which, like the 'pale primroses', is nevertheless threatened by circumstances.

I think we *must* care about our physical world, the Earth herself and the lives of those who live on it. Given the choice between non-realist life people and world people, I'd opt for being among the world people, who are concerned about the real world, but a better name for what we are and must be is Earth people. Goddesses and Gods are not real. Calling the Earth a Mother Goddess is a poetic trope of super-naturalisation. It is telling us something about the Earth in a *poetic* way. But the Earth herself *is* real and so are her inhabitants including ourselves. It is unwise to be 'non-realist' about our physical reality, to discount it as unimportant. If we feel superior to what is going on in the real world and can't be bothered to concern ourselves with it, we may act very unwisely or fail to do what we should and become complicit by default.

As we said above, postmodernist 'non-realism' about the Earth is the ideal partner for an aggressive capitalism that *commodifies* the Earth and reduces it to nothing but money. One of the major obstacles to getting a satisfactory world agreement on the environment and to combating climate change is the power of large corporate interests to stall and block it, particularly in the USA.

As we said in the previous chapter, poetry must be distinguished from science and ethics. It is for the scientists to tell us what is happening to our environment on Earth and whether we are endangering our habitat. Given this knowledge, it is for ethics to work out what we should do and for politics to try and achieve it. But we also said another function of poetry is to *warn*. Poetry can express the anxiety we feel as ordinary mortals when we hear that the Earth is in danger. Poetry can *imagine* what a destroyed Earth would be like. Poetry can remind us how beautiful the Earth is and mortal beauty, says Hopkins, 'keeps warm men's wits'. This warm glow may make us feel it is unfitting and wrong that cruelty and evil should exist in such a beautiful world. It does not *necessarily* impel us to do anything about it or to be kinder ourselves.

Nevertheless, beauty can foster love and love can bring forth action. So we do need the poetic mode of apprehending the Earth. It is vital to combat the silly postmodernism that regards the Earth as 'non-real' and therefore unimportant, and the aggressive commercialism that is prepared to allow the Earth to perish, provided it makes a profit. We need the poet's 'enlarged and numerous senses' to treat the Earth with reverence, and awe, as a living ecosphere, as holy. Calling the Earth a Great Mother, a Goddess, is a poetic device con-tributing to this task.

A Closer Look at the Mother Metaphor

Like every poetic trope using symbolic language – metaphor, personification, supernaturalisation – the comparison of the Earth to a 'Great Mother' corresponds in some respects but not others. In all these poetic tropes, we said, *vehicle* and *tenor* are not 100% alike or they would be identical. When I say, metaphorically, 'David is a lion', I mean the man David is like a lion in some respects. If I go to the zoo and meet a live lion and give him the name David, that is not a metaphor.

The Earth is a mother to us, because we derive our being from her. We belong to her whole evolving ecosphere. In that sense we are Earth's children. Secondly, all through our lives, the Earth sustains us, provides us with food and shelter. We cannot live without her. As we discuss later in this chapter, monotheistic religions – Judaism, Christianity, Islam – worship a single *male* deity and have suppressed the Great Mother. However, she has to some extent re-established herself in Catholicism in the cult of Mary as Mother of God – θεοτοχος *(theotokos)* – and later in this chapter we will also see how Mary has sometimes been identified with the original Great Goddess. It is therefore not surprising that many distinguished eco-theologians, who have stressed our need to reverence and care for the Earth, are or were Catholics. Names such as Teilhard de Chardin, Thomas Berry and Matthew Fox spring to mind. On the other hand, the official Catholic church uses its theology of Nature to preach the most damaging ethical doctrines, such as its ban on contraception and on condoms used to prevent the spread of AIDS. Certainly, contraception is 'unnatural' but it is obviously better for a woman and for the planet as a whole if she can control her own fertility. And to hear the Pope condemning condoms in Africa, where AIDS is epidemic, made one want to weep with fury.

Modern ecologists and eco-theologians have called the Earth Gaia, the name of the Greek Earth goddess, the primordial Great Mother. For example, in his book *Coming Back to Earth: From gods to God to Gaia*,[39] the New Zealand theologian Lloyd Geering advocates that we should return to the worship of Gaia, treat the Earth with the reverence due to a goddess and look after her. But tellingly, he says that Gaia was the wife of Zeus (Latin: Jupiter). In fact, Gaia was Zeus' grandmother and very promiscuous. Her first children were born by parthenogenesis. Then she had a lot more by her son Uranus *(ouranos* = sky), including Cronos the father of Zeus, and countless other children by other fathers, one of whom was her grandson Zeus. Zeus' own official consort was the more decorous Hera. Perhaps those who fulminate against

---

[39] Lloyd Geering, *Coming Back to Earth: From gods to God to Gaia* (Polebridge Press, Salem, USA 2009).

'feckless' unmarried mothers have the same punitive instincts as the ancient Israelites, who destroyed the shrines of the ancient Canaanite Earth goddess to impose their single male deity.

Mother Nature has countless children and some of them live and more of them die. In his poem *In Memoriam,* published in 1849, ten years before Darwin's *Origin of Species,* Tennyson calls Nature 'red in tooth and claw'. He accuses her:

> Are God and Nature then at strife,
> That Nature tends such evil dreams?
> So careful of the type, she seems
> So careless of the single life.

He goes on to say:

> So careful of the type? but no.
> From scarped cliff and quarried stone
> She cries: A thousand types are gone:
> I care for nothing, all shall go.[40]

On the other hand, human mothers are not usually that careless. Most mothers look after their babies in a way the Earth does not. They listen to their infant, delight in how each child is different, get to know each individual child very intimately, elicit language from him or her, not only giving the child to the world but the world to the child. Of course, human mothers could not exist or do any of these things if Earth had not evolved them in the first place. But we should not *reduce* human mothers to nothing but 'Earth mothers'. Human mothers do much more than giving birth and sustaining their children. Human mothers can *speak*, whereas

---

[40] *In Memoriam*, 55, 56.

the Earth cannot. And many human mothers do a lot more than childcare. They are not *nothing but* mothers. They work, create other things, because they have to, need to or want to…

Lastly, another way in which Earth is not like a human mother is that human children grow up and have to detach themselves from their mothers and fathers. They must become adults, independent of their parents and may end up looking after their elderly parents. That is not the case with the Earth. No creature living on Earth can ever become independent of her. Perhaps it was a muddle about this metaphor that led people to think we *could* become independent of the Earth through Enlightenment, or 'the white heat of technology', because humanity had 'come of age'. When we call the Earth our mother, we must remember that motherhood is not all sweetness and light, and that the Earth as Mother and human beings as mothers differ in certain crucial respects.

Father

The three monotheistic religions, Judaism, Christianity and Islam, have a single male God. Yahweh the God of the ancient Israelites was originally a tribal god who delivered his people from slavery in Egypt, and a Sky Father who dwelt in the heavens. When the people of Israel entered the promised land of Canaan they suppressed the nature gods and goddesses, including the Great Mother Goddess, of the local inhabitants and gradually imposed their single male god. In the Old Testament Yahweh is sometimes called father,[41] but this is not how he is usually addressed. It is Jesus who constantly speaks of his Father, whom he does address as 'Abba' (meaning father, or even 'Daddy'), and who teaches his followers to

---

[41] e.g. Deut 32: 6; Ps 88: 27; Ps 103: 13; Is 63: 16; Hos 11: 1.

pray: 'Our Father who art in heaven'. (Incidentally, in every reported conversation of Jesus with his mother, apart from his words from the cross in John, he is off-hand, even rude to her.)

This God the Father is held to be the creator of the world and as such, praise which had been given to Mother Nature becomes due to him. God the Father also comes to be regarded as the supreme source of values: he is Love, Goodness, Life, Being etc. When God is thought of as Love itself, Goodness itself, questions arise about why he allows bad things to happen, 'the problem of evil'. So his two roles as world creator and source of all moral value do not always sit easily together.

Like the Great Mother Goddess, God the Father is a creation of the human imagination by means of the poetic trope of *supernaturalisation* of forces and potential to be found in the cosmos and ourselves. Here is one more Other Way Round insight we spoke about in the Introduction. Rather than 'the Father of our Lord Jesus Christ, from whom all fatherhood in heaven and Earth takes its name',[42] it is our human experience of fatherhood from which we project a Heavenly Father. Likewise with all the virtues. Virtues are about *doing*: they are verbs. Our – sometimes not very successful – attempts at loving, being/doing good, living well are not pale shadows of a supernatural Subsistent Love, Goodness, Life (all abstract *nouns)* but are what enable us to project these virtues – perfected – onto a Supernatural Ideal.

There is no need to personify or supernaturalise these virtues in a Perfect Being. That is a poetic way of formulating an *idea* of what these virtues mean or entail. There is also no

---

[42] Eph 3: 14.

need to supernaturalise the energy that created the cosmos at the beginning of time with the Big Bang and say that energy itself was created by Something or Someone outside time altogether. This does not solve the problem, because it could lead to an infinite regression of 'who created the creator'. So one might just as well stick to the facts of the natural world as far as scientists can establish them (an exercise that is never final). The cosmos itself says – is – I AM; we can praise the cosmos itself:

> Look at the stars! Look, look up at the skies!
> O look at all the fire-folk sitting in the air!
> The bright boroughs, the circle-citadels there![43]

I think the metaphor created by the human poetic genius of a Father God is still powerful in two ways. Firstly as 'Sky Father'. This is a way of acknowledging that I did *not* create the cosmos. It existed long before me and after a long process of evolution, I came into being as one of the transient living beings that this cosmos has produced. Secondly, our Father can stand for 'the fathers that begat us': our *cultural* ancestors. As Lloyd Geering puts it in his essay 'Saving the Planet':[44]

> In learning to value the totality of human culture and spirituality, we also come to realise how dependent we are on our own cultural inheritance. In the past, our spiritual forebears felt themselves to be dependent on the will and activity of God, the supreme supernatural being. For us that feeling of dependence on God has been replaced by a feeling of dependence on the countless generations before us who helped to create the culture we inherited. What our forebears once attributed to the creativity of the divine heavenly creator, we must now attribute to our cultural ancestors and *with a similar degree of gratitude.*

---

[43] G.M. Hopkins, 'The Starlight Night'.
[44] In *Time and Tide* (O Books, Alresford, Hants 2001), p. 83.

Many indigenous religions include ancestor worship. We honour our cultural ancestors, for example in the blue plaques on London houses, celebration of anniversaries such as Milton's 400th birthday celebrations at Chalfont St Giles in 2008, by tombstones and monuments, and, above all, by reading their works. (Actually, people today often prefer the biographies, but perhaps that is a sign of our mental laziness.) Our cultural ancestors are also women and we honour them too, for example in the celebrations for Mary Wollstonecraft's 250th birthday in Old St Pancras church in 2009. Her words were read out in the church and a splendid birthday cake was cut on a table put up by her tombstone.

We receive our life from our parents and ultimately from the energy of the cosmos; we inherit our culture from our ancestors. We can be grateful to the cosmos and our cultural forebears for what we have received, with what could be called *filial* gratitude. In our lifetime we may hope to pass on the life we have received to children or contribute to the culture we have inherited.

Many fathers not only generate their children biologically but love them and do their best to provide for them. It is good for children to grow up with both a loving mother and a loving father. Jesus compares God to such a father, for example in the parable of the Prodigal Son.[45] The son goes off and 'squanders his property in loose living'. When he is destitute he decides to go home and throw himself upon his father's mercy. His father sees him coming and

> ran and embraced him and kissed him. And the son said to him: 'Father I have sinned against heaven and before you; I am no longer worthy to be called your son.' But the father

---

[45] Lk 15: 11–32.

said to his servants, 'Bring quickly the best robe, and put it on him; and put a ring on his hand, and shoes on his feet; and bring the fatted calf and kill it, and let us eat and make merry; for this my son was dead and is alive again; he was lost and is found.' And they began to make merry.

This is a beautiful picture of a loving father. There is one odd feature in it, though: the complete absence of the mother.

God the Father is praised as the creator of the cosmos. The Nicene Creed begins:

> I believe in one God, the Father Almighty, Maker of heaven and Earth, and of all things visible and invisible.

The *Canticle of the Creatures* ascribed to St Francis proclaims:

> All praise be yours, my Lord,
> through all that you have made,
> and first Sir Brother Sun, who brings the day;
> and through whom you give us light.
> And he is beautiful and radiant with great splendour;
> of you, Most High, he bears the likeness.
> All praise be yours, my Lord, through Sister Moon
> and the stars, in the heavens you have made them,
> bright, precious and fair...

In another prayer ascribed to St Francis God the Father is praised as the source of all the virtues:

> You are holy, Lord, the only God, and your deeds are wonderful. You are strong. You are great. You are the Most High. You are Almighty. You, Holy Father, are King of heaven and Earth... You are Good, all Good, supreme Good, Lord God, living and true. You are love. You are wisdom. You are humility. You are endurance. You are rest. You are peace. You are joy and gladness...

God the Father, the historical God of Israel, is praised for liberating his people from slavery and saving his people again in a new covenant sealed in the blood of Jesus. In the words of the well-known hymn:

> Praise my soul, the King of heaven,
> To his feet thy tribute bring;
> Ransomed, healed, restored, forgiven,
> Who like me his praise should sing…

> Praise him for his grace and favour
> To our fathers in distress;
> Praise him still the same for ever,
> Slow to chide and swift to bless…

> Father-like he tends and spares us…

There are countless songs, poems, psalms, liturgies praising God the Father. Many (not all) are very beautiful and have 'passed into the fabric of the mind' of a Christian culture. There is no room to quote much more. But here is George Herbert praising God for creating and kindly maintaining the cosmic *order*. A single God calling himself I AM, who 'fathered' the whole cosmos, through his word or wisdom, is a poetic way of conceiving an ordered *universe,* governed by physical laws, making modern science possible. The cosmic order is mirrored in Herbert's poem 'Paradise', not only in its regular four-beat lines and three-line stanzas, but in its playful (and strict) rhyme-scheme in which one letter is successively removed from the rhyming word:

> I bless thee, Lord, because I GROW
> Among thy trees, which in a ROW
> To thee both fruit and order OW.

What open force, or hidden CHARM
Can blast my fruit, or bring me HARM,
While the inclosure is thine ARM?

The Dark Father

However, the 'God the Father' metaphor is apt only up to a point. Or rather, fatherhood itself has light and dark sides. Jesus portrays God as a caring Father, who cares for every hair on our heads:

> Are not two sparrows sold for a penny? Yet not one of them will fall to the ground unperceived by your Father. And even the hairs of your head are all counted. So don't be afraid; you are worth more than many sparrows.[46]

And:

> Is there anyone among you who, if your child asks for bread, will give him a stone? Or if the child asks for a fish, will give a snake? If you then, who are evil, know how to give good gifts to your children, how much more will your Father in heaven give good things to those who ask him![47]

Jesus is clearly wrong about what often happens. There are many people in the world without bread, who pray and beg for it and still starve. Others suffer terrible pain, which is not relieved, however hard they pray. Sometimes it seems appropriate to picture God as a caring Father, but sometimes he seems more like an absent or cruel father. Human fathers can be all these things: loving, caring, providing, absent, indifferent, abusive; fathers are much more likely to abandon, harm or kill their children than mothers. The cosmos originates life and contains everything that is needed to sustain

---

[46] Mt 10: 29.
[47] Mt 7: 9.

human life in general, but the cosmos doesn't care. As Hopkins puts it in *The Wreck of the Deutschland*:

> O Father, not under thy feathers nor ever as guessing
> The goal was a shoal, of a fourth the doom to be drowned.

The Deutschland sets out into a storm when 'the infinite air is unkind' and:

> Wiry and white-fiery and whirlwind-swivellèd snow
> Spins to the widow-making unchilding unfathering deeps.

And then we have the Agony in the Garden. Jesus prays: 'Father, if you are willing, take away this cup from me; yet, not my will, but yours be done.'[48] Jesus believes his Father *wants* him to go through horrible pain and death, and accepts his Father's will. 'And his sweat became like great drops of blood falling down upon the ground.' What kind of a father wants that, does that to his child? Certainly not a very good father in our eyes. When a father kills his children we think of that act as monstrous. The male monotheist punitive Father of a certain Christian theology of the atonement has done much damage.

Abraham, who was willing to sacrifice his son Isaac, is regarded as a 'type' of God the Father sacrificing his son. According to George Frazer in *The Golden Bough*,[49] it was the practice among the Semites of Western Asia for the king sometimes to sacrifice his son in times of national danger. And in the Old Testament[50] we have the story of the king of Moab, who sacrificed his son to stave off defeat in battle by Israel *and it worked*:

---

[48] Lk 22: 42.
[49] 1922.
[50] 2 Kings 3.

Now Mesha King of Moab was a sheep breeder and he had to deliver annually to the king of Israel a hundred thousand lambs, and the wool of a hundred thousand rams.

When Moab rebels against this heavy tribute, King Jehoram of Israel, together with Jehosaphat of Judah and the king of Edom, march against him. At the end of the story:

> When the king of Moab saw that the battle was going against him, he took with him seven hundred swordsmen to break through, opposite the king of Edom, but they could not. Then he took his firstborn son who was to succeed him, and offered him for a burnt offering on the wall. And great wrath came upon Israel, so they withdrew from him and returned to their own land.

By sacrificing his son, the king saved his people.

Human fathers may regard their children as their property. As journalist Deborah Orr writes in a report on child-murder-father-suicide cases:[51] 'Some fathers cannot recognise their children other than as extensions of themselves.' She quotes a string of cases in which men have killed themselves and their children. One father left a note for his estranged wife: 'I am taking mine with me.' Child-murder-parental-suicide cases almost always involve the father. Of course, the vast majority of fathers do not kill or harm their children.

God the Father is also seen as *owning* us his children. I have often wondered about the Father in the Pauline drama of the cosmic Christ. For example, he writes to the Corinthians:

> Then the end will come, when Christ hands over the kingdom to God the Father, after he has destroyed every

---

[51] *Independent,* 16th July 2002.

ruler and every authority and power... For 'God has put all things in subjection under his feet.' But when it says: 'All things are put in subjection', it is plain that this does not include the one who put all things in subjection under him. When all things are subjected to him, *the Son himself will also be subjected* to the one who put all things in subjection under him, so that God may be all in all. [52]

That is not what sons usually do. They usually grow up and *supersede* their fathers. A son who always remains subject to his father is not an adult. I have eventually come to the conclusion that the answer lies in another Pauline concept: that of Christ's body, a whole humanity as 'the fullness of Christ'. Then the finale of his great sweeping cosmic drama would be Christ the Son as humanity's 'namesake hero' *taking over* from his Father. An adult humanity cannot remain *subject* to its father; we have to take our own decisions and not rely on God to help us out. God in that sense is dead. As Thomas Hardy wrote in his poem 'God's Funeral' almost exactly a hundred years ago:

> O man-projected Figure, of late
> Imaged as we, thy knell who shall survive?
> Whence came it we were tempted to create
> One whom we can no longer keep alive? ...
>
> And, tricked by our own early dream
> And need of solace, we grew self-deceived,
> Our making soon our maker did we deem,
> And what we had imagined we believed.

Nevertheless, not just at its birth but day by day until its end, life continues to be something we *receive*. In one sense an adult humanity takes over moral responsibility from God the Father, but we never take over from the cosmos. We remain

---

[52] 1 Cor 15: 24.

dependent on it and on our own Earth. If we keep 'God the Father' as a metaphor for the cosmos which generates and sustains us, and for our cultural heritage from previous generations, it is a metaphor that applies in quite a complex way, bringing out positive and negative aspects of fatherhood, as are found in human fathers.

The metaphor of God the Father, as the author of our being and of the whole cosmos from which we evolved, expresses the idea of a *universe*, a single cosmic order, which we can greet with awe and praise. That conception of a cosmic *order*, rather than a plethora of wilful gods and goddesses, is what made modern science possible. However, as we saw, the triumph of God the Father suppressed the Great Mother Goddess, so that this Father is praised for *making* everything on Earth, rather than the Earth praised for herself. Both the Father God and the Mother Goddess are metaphors or supernaturalisations, but suppressing the female has led to problems and distortions.

Some theologians and ecologists have blamed male monotheism with its accompanying suppression of the Earth Mother Goddess for lack of respect for the Earth and the ecological crisis that is currently upon us. God the Father has also been used to prop up a patriarchal system, in which women are subjugated and often oppressed and abused. Female sexuality has been feared and demonised. A male clergy that bosses women about and rules over their lives is an ugly phenomenon; a celibate male clergy that does so is both ugly and bizarre. And when that so-called celibate male clergy abuses children, in Jesus' words: 'It would be better for him to have a great millstone fastened round his neck and to be drowned in the depth of the sea.'[53]

---

[53]   Mt 18: 6.

Sexuality is the power that has enabled life to evolve into more complex forms and vastly increased its richness and variety. The poetry of Earth and cosmos involves both male and female and there is much more to praise when we acknowledge *both*. If for our praise and reverence we want to keep our poetic trope of supernaturalisation, it makes more sense to keep both a Great God and a Great Goddess. Perhaps that is why in some indigenous religions the Supreme Being is both male and female; for example, the Toltec Ometeotl is the 'Lord and Lady of Duality'.

In chapter 3, we look at the Making of Humanity in the Christ Epic but before that we go on a Mexican excursion in search of the Great Mother in Guadalupe Tonantzin. As we noted, even within orthodox Catholicism, the lack of a female deity was strongly felt and when Jesus' mother Mary was named God-bearer, mother of God – θεοτοκος *(theotokos)* – at the Council of Ephesus in 431, she began to fulfil that role (though she never officially became divine). Our Mexican excursion gives an example of how Mary became identified with the indigenous Earth Goddess. On the other hand, Protestant theology suppressed the cult of Mary and perhaps that denial of reverence for the female facilitated the rise of capitalism, which can lead to a quest to dominate the Earth and exploit it for profit at any cost.

A Mexican Excursion:

Guadalupe Tonantzin – 'Our Mother'

Background

In 1492, after the Muslim Moors were finally driven out of Spain, the Catholic monarchs Ferdinand and Isabella sent Columbus on an expedition which reached the 'West Indies', in fact Caribbean islands, not, as he supposed, the Asian mainland. This led to the opening up of a New World, which Spain proceeded to colonise both for its wealth and to spread Christianity. In 1519 Hernán Cortés set out from Cuba with a small expedition of about 500 men and landed at Vera Cruz on the Mexican mainland Yucatán Peninsula. By 1521 he had conquered and destroyed the magnificent Aztec city of Tenochtitlán (now Mexico City) – then a much larger city than any in Europe with a population estimated at over 200,000; by comparison Henry VIII's London probably had a population of about 55,000.

How did Cortés conquer the great Aztec Empire so easily? From the large literature on this subject, we may briefly mention the following points. Firstly, the Spaniards had superior warfare technology, including gunpowder and horses, which the indigenous people had never seen. They also brought diseases, such as smallpox, from which the indigenous people had no immunity. Secondly, the rapidly expanding Aztec Empire was hated by the neighbouring tribes they had conquered because they exacted heavy tribute and captives for human sacrifice. Cortés succeeded in forming alliances with some of these tribes, such as the Tlaxcalans, who helped him conquer the Aztecs. Thirdly, the Aztec Emperor Moctezuma may have thought the Spaniards were the legendary god-king

Quetzalcoatl, who had disappeared into the sea but promised to return.

Quetzalcoatl had been the historical king of a previous Mexican high civilisation, the Toltecs, who were famous artists, craftsmen and poets. King Quetzalcoatl was also the priest of a single god whose name was Quetzalcoatl too, a manifestation of Ometeotl, the 'Divine Pair' – supreme god both male and female – the 'Lord and Lady of Duality'. King Quetzalcoatl was driven out of the city for forbidding human sacrifice and disappeared into the sea. At this point he leaves history and enters into myth (in some versions of the story he becomes the evening and then the morning star: Venus).

The Aztec barbarians invading from the North rapidly assimilated the achievements of their more civilised predecessors and also took over their gods, so that their pantheon became very large and complex. They forgot Quetzalcoatl's ban on human sacrifice and their most-revered god became the bloodthirsty sun and war god Huitzilopochtli, who demanded a constant supply of victims so that the sun would not fail. However, a resistance group of *tlamantinimes* continued to oppose human sacrifice and honour the tradition of Quetzalcoatl.

In some ways the Spaniards were like the Aztecs, being prepared to kill thousands in the name of their god. But unlike the Aztecs, the Spaniards were not syncretists: they thought their god was not only the top god, but the only god, and all the others were demons who should be exterminated. They smashed as many shrines as possible of the indigenous gods and not only killed thousands of native inhabitants but did their best to destroy their religion and culture.

The Appearances of 'Our Mother'

In December 1531, ten years after the destruction of the city of Tenochtitlán, a poor indigenous man, who had been converted to Christianity by the Spaniards and given the Christian name Juan Diego, was on his way to church and passing the hill of Tepeyac on the outskirts of what is now Mexico City. Tepeyac was the holy hill of the indigenous great mother goddess Tonantzin (which means 'Our Mother'). On Tepeyac Juan Diego encountered a Lady, dark-skinned, indigenous and very beautiful. She spoke to Juan Diego in Nahuatl, his mother tongue. She tells him: 'I am the Ever Virgin Holy Mary, Mother of Great Truth, *Teotl Dios* ['God' in Nahuatl and Spanish]; Mother of the Life-Giver, *Ipalnemohuani*; Mother of the Creator of Humanity, *Teyocoyani*; Mother of the Lord of the Near and Together, *Tloque Nahuaque*; Mother of the Lord of Heaven and Earth, *in Ilhicahua in Tlalticpaque.*' She identifies herself with both the Christian Mother Mary and the indigenous Mother Goddess and equates the two. She asks Juan Diego to go to the bishop and say she would like her holy house built on Tepeyac Hill.

The story is told in the *Nican Mopohua*,[54] a poem written in Nahuatl (the Aztec language). According to Nahuatl expert Miguel León Portilla, the poem was most probably written in 1556 by the Nahuatl native speaker Antonio Valeriano, who was a student at the Santa Cruz College founded by the Spaniards at Tlatelolco, where the students became trilingual in Nahuatl, Spanish and Latin. The poem goes on to tell how at first the Spanish bishop Juan de Zumárraga did not believe

---

[54] *Guadalupe Mother of the New Creation* by Virgil Elizondo (Orbis Books, New York 1997) has an English translation of the full text of the *Nican Mopohua*. Miguel León Portilla's *Tonantzin Guadalupe* (El Colegio Nacional: Fondo de Cultura Económica, Mexico 2000) has the full Nahuatl version with Spanish translation.

73

the poor Indian Juan Diego (who belonged to the *macehual* class of 'commoners'), but finally became convinced on Juan Diego's third visit by the out-of-season flowers the Lady had told him to gather on the cold top of Tepeyac Hill, which he carried to the bishop's Palace in his poncho or *tilma*. When he opened the *tilma* to show the flowers, it bore the Lady's miraculous image on it. A house, later a large church, was built on Tepeyac Hill in honour of the Lady, whom the Spaniards called Our Lady of Guadalupe and the indigenous people continued to call Tonantzin. By 1556 large crowds of both Indians and Spaniards regularly came to honour the Lady at Tepeyac and have done so ever since.

In the poem the Lady not only appears as an ordinary dark-skinned indigenous woman and speaks to Juan Diego in his Nahuatl mother tongue, but she treats him with affection and respect, as an equal. (She speaks to him standing up; if she had been a noble, she would have received him sitting down.) She addresses him in familiar language, using many diminutives, like a mother. The indigenous Nahuatl people had seen their world destroyed, their great capital city in ruins, their culture and religion smashed. An estimated population of 25 million when the Spaniards arrived declined by the end of the century to one million, from conquest, disease and suicide. The psychological trauma must have been devastating. But the Lady tells Juan Diego she is the Mother of *both* the Christian god (*Dios*) and the supreme Nahuatl god and she repeats some of that god's highest titles (Life-Giver, Creator of Humanity, Lord of the Near and Together, Lord of Heaven and Earth). When Juan Diego says he is of too humble status to speak to the bishop, she insists he is her chosen messenger and he ends up carrying the good news to the bishop ('evangelising' him). The Lady represents the female aspect of the divinity, the nurturing Earth Mother. She tells Juan Diego: 'I am your kind mother and the mother of all the nations that live on this

Earth who would love me.' She accords the poor equal, or even greater, dignity than the rich and equally assumes both Christian and Nahuatl names of the great 'Life-Giver'.

The sixteenth-century Franciscan friar Bernardino de Sahagún condemned the cult of the Lady at Tepeyac as an undercover continuation of the old religion at a Christian shrine, and others since then have repeated that condemnation. On the other hand, some called it a Christian plot to 'subsume' and thereby overcome the cult of the indigenous Tonantzin and replace her with Mary. Nevertheless, today an estimated 10 million worshippers visit her Basilica annually – still whispering, 'Tonantzin Guadalupe, hear our prayers' (with no difficulty combining them) – making it the most popular shrine to 'Our Lady' in the world.

Guadalupe in Mexican History

Our Lady of Guadalupe became closely bound up with struggles for Mexican independence and identity, including the struggles of the indigenous population. In the war of Mexican independence from Spain (1810–21) the rebels' banner had her image on it and their rallying cry was: *¡Viva la Virgen de Guadalupe! ¡Viva la Independencia!* Manuel Felix Fernández, the first President of independent Mexico, changed his name to Guadalupe Victoria. During the Mexican Revolution (1910–1920) followers of Zapata (mainly indigenous peasants) also called upon Our Lady of Guadalupe and their rallying cry was: Land and Freedom! They demanded agrarian reform and redistribution of the agricultural land owned by the great rich landowners. It seemed natural to them to call upon the Lady who had appeared to Juan Diego; she represented Mother Earth, was an indigenous commoner and chose an indigenous commoner for her messenger. It is not surprising that for theologians like Virgil Elizondo[55] she is a major figure in liberation theology.

Guadalupe and the Zapatistas Today

In 1994 the Zapatistas, who are mainly Mayan Indians from the Lacandon Jungle in Chiapas, South-East Mexico, rose up and briefly took control of the nearby small city and bishopric, San Cristóbal de las Casas, in protest against NAFTA, the newly ratified North American Free Trade Agreement, which massively benefits large US corporations against the Mexican poor and indigenous. The Zapatistas were also demanding land rights and some autonomy. They retreated to their jungle and named their first Zapatista base Guadalupe Tepeyac, because this Lady, an indigenous woman like themselves, had proclaimed herself mother of all. As Tonantzin she is Mother Earth and these poor Mayan peasants claimed their share of the Earth's bounty. In their culture they treat the Earth as holy and there are lessons to be learnt from them about sustainable agriculture.

According to Luke in the New Testament, the pregnant Mary is the first to proclaim the gospel in her song, the Magnificat: the mighty put down from their seats and the poor raised up, the hungry filled with good things and the rich sent empty away. (Incidentally, Bach's *Magnificat in D* is very expressive and attentive to the meaning.) Mary gives birth in a lowly stable to Jesus, 'a saviour who is Christ the Lord', as the angel told the shepherds. The humble shepherds are the first to hear about it, just as the poor indigenous Juan Diego was the one chosen to receive the Lady of Guadalupe's message. In Luke's Gospel Mary's son Jesus says plainly: 'Blessed are the poor' (not 'poor in spirit' as in Matthew) for yours is the

---

[55] See *Guadalupe Mother of the New Creation*.

reign of God and 'Blessed are the hungry' (for food) for you will be filled.

The struggle for land is real and continuing. To give just one example, a self-styled environmental group called Conservation International, sponsored by many large multinational corporations including Citigroup, Exxon Mobil and McDonald's, and closely linked with Starbucks in exporting token amounts of organic coffee from the Montes Azules region of the Lacandon Jungle, has made concerted efforts to clear the Zapatistas from the area. Its activities include bio-prospecting for private-sector partners (which may involve biopiracy for pharmaceutical companies); it has bought the right to set up a genetic research station in Montes Azules and has co-operated with the Mexican government in a repressive military campaign against the Zapatistas, whom the Mexican government has described as an 'international security matter' and a problem of 'serious ungovernability'. Conservation International's programme of flyovers – part of the USAID-supported international monitoring programme – uses state-of-the-art geographical information systems technology, including high-resolution satellite imaging, which could be used to identify the location of natural resources attractive to commercial interests. A June 2003 report by the Mexican Chiapas-based Centre for Political Analysis and Social Investigation dubbed Conservation International 'a Trojan horse of the US government and transnational corporations'. And other independent agencies have described the 'environmental' concerns of the Mexican and US governments in the Lacandon Jungle as being military and geostrategic 'alibis'.

In 1995 the Mexican army smashed Guadalupe Tepeyac and the Zapatistas were driven out of their first base. Guadalupe Tepeyac now became a 'migratory' community and in a communiqué of March 1995 (published in *La Jornada* and other Mexican newspapers, and posted on the internet)[56] their leader, Subcomandante Marcos, gives a humorous description of a long discussion they have when someone from the city has sent them a present of an image of Our Lady of Guadalupe:

> A few days ago in the now 'migratory' village of Guadalupe Tepeyac, there was an argument. A gift came to them from the city. Among the scant humanitarian aid they receive, the 'Guadalupan Zapatistas' (as they call themselves) found an image of the Virgin of Guadalupe. From what they tell me, the image measures about 30 centimetres, has some golden cords and coloured candles.

They decide to hold a general assembly to discuss whether the image should go with them when they try to go home, or whether it should stay in their present host village. Marcos continues:

> Doña Herminia begins to clear her throat. Everyone falls silent. This means that the foundress of Guadalupe Tepeyac, and its oldest inhabitant, is about to speak. With the weight of her hundred years, Doña Herminia begins to speak slowly and quietly... She says that the Virgin of Guadalupe has come again from the city to find her sons and daughters, the Guadalupan Zapatistas, and as she did not find them at home she searched for them uphill and downhill, and reached them after much travelling up and down from one place to another.

---

56 Zapatista communiqués are posted on:
http://enlacezapatista.ezln.org.mx
(Spanish with some English translations. A search will produce other sites with English translations.) *Zapatista Stories,* a collection of stories by Subcomandante Marcos, translated by Dinah Livingstone, was published by Katabasis in 2001.

She says that the Virgin must be tired of so much trudging up and down, especially in this heat that dries up saints and sinners alike, that a little rest would do her no harm at all and that now she is with them it's good that the Virgin should rest a while with her own. But she ('mother Lupita') did not come from so far away to stay here, she didn't travel all over the place looking for us, just to stay here in this place if the Guadalupan Zapatistas leave it and go somewhere else.

Doña Herminia thinks (and here all the women and the odd man nod in agreement) that the Lady of Guadalupe will want to be with her sons and daughters wherever they are, and that her tiredness will lessen if she rests together with them, her family, and her sadness will hurt her less if she suffers together with them, and joy will shine out more if it shines on her with them.

Doña Herminia says she thinks (and now there are more who agree) that the Virgin will want to go wherever the people of Guadalupe Tepeyac go, that if the war drives them into the mountains, to the mountains the Virgin will go, turned soldier like them, to defend her dark dignity; that if peace brings them back to their homes, the Lady of Guadalupe will go with them to the village to rebuild what was destroyed.

'So I ask you, *madrecita* [little mother], if you agree to going where we go...' she asks, addressing the image that is in front of the assembly. The Virgin doesn't answer, her dark gaze keeps on looking down... The assembly leader asks if anyone else wants to speak. There is a unanimous silence. 'There will be a vote,' he says, and takes the vote. The women win. The Virgin of Guadalupe will go wherever the Guadalupan Zapatistas go. After the assembly there will be a dance. A marimba and the dark-skinned image preside over the party.

Marcos' attitude to the image is one of affectionate respect but he in no way treats her as supernatural. In a similar vein, he often recounts stories about the old Mayan gods. Marcos knows that Our Lady of Guadalupe is an immensely important symbol of a real struggle for a just share of the Earth's wealth, as a mother providing for all her children. He is able to joke about her in a light-hearted way, but knows her symbolic power operates for those who do not think she is supernatural, as well as for those who do. He is an 'object lesson' in discerning and absorbing the wisdom of traditional religious stories and symbols, without pretending that they are anything but 'poetic tales'.

On the other hand, in 2002, boasting that this was the Catholic church's first indigenous saint, Pope John Paul II canonised Juan Diego, to whom the Lady of Guadalupe appeared. The Pope did not mention the fact that Juan Diego may not actually have existed; he is the hero of a poem!

In exploring religion as a human creation we can learn from Marcos' affectionate respect to discern the wisdom in old religious stories and traditions. But we should not be uncritical. Just because a religion is 'ethnic' or 'exotic' does not mean we should 'lay off' out of a misguided multicultural 'correctness', tolerate it as 'quaint' or treat it with 'folksy' acceptance. All religious traditions must be judged by humanist criteria. For example, in his poem *Quetzalcoatl,* Ernesto Cardenal roundly denounces the horrendous human sacrifices practised by the Aztecs, whom he regards as a more barbaric culture succeeding the high culture of the Toltecs. He describes the resistance of the *tlamantinimes,* who continued to oppose human sacrifice and honour the tradition of Quetzalcoatl, as *anti-fascist.*

And if we oppose human sacrifice in the religion of the Aztecs, a former American superpower, we must continue to oppose it today. The USA, the present American superpower, has parallels with the Aztecs. The Aztecs practised human sacrifice to keep the sun burning. The USA has engaged in wars in Afghanistan and Iraq, in which the geopolitics of oil are a major factor. Over a million people have died, sacrificed in the Iraq war and its aftermath. As well as learning from the wisdom of old religious traditions, we can learn from their *un*wisdom and become part of the resistance to human sacrifice.

We can also learn from 'Our Mother' Tonantzin Guadalupe that the Earth is alive and should be treated with reverence, not over-exploited, poisoned and endangered; she is mother to all and her wealth must be fairly shared. We cannot say the West has achieved the realisation of Christianity when so many people are still poor, hungry and dispossessed, for which Western capitalism bears a large responsibility. 'Our Mother's' Magnificat 'raises up the lowly' and 'fills the hungry with good things'. Not with any old rubbish, but with *good things*.

Chapter 3

Earthchild: The Making of Humanity

Grand Narrative

Fashionable philosophers tell us that just because God is not real, this means that humanity is not real either. That seems a silly idea to me. The two cases are quite different. The supernatural realm is a human poetic creation, but humanity is human beings. There are billions of real human beings on Earth, who are very much alive. Many human beings also really lived and died in the past. So what about Grand Narrative? By that we mean a story about the whole trajectory of humanity: where humanity is going, its destiny, what would constitute its fulfilment, salvation, liberation. Postmodernists also keep telling us that Grand Narrative is dead. Twenty years ago communism collapsed: the Marxist story of the coming of a just society through the dictatorship of the proletariat. In that story the proletariat is the engine of history and history itself is a kind of *deus ex machina* – a sort of god if you like – with scientific laws that make the glorious end of the story inevitable. Although the Soviet Union never really embodied that vision and was not really a communist society, its collapse discredited communism and its Grand Narrative.

The Christian Grand Narrative of the coming of a just society has also been discredited. As we do not believe in inevitable scientific laws of history as a *deus ex machina*, neither do we believe in the agency of supernatural beings to bring about the desired goal. In the New Testament we find two or perhaps three related 'takes' or versions of the Grand Narrative of the good society: Jesus preaching the kingdom of God, the reign of justice and peace on Earth; and the Christ Epic with its twin story of humanity as one single body, the body of Christ, *and* the story of the marriage of heaven and Earth with Christ as the bridegroom. In all these stories God *acts* and human fulfilment is brought about through his agency. Like many of us today in Britain, Europe and elsewhere, I find it impossible to believe in a supernatural agency. I don't think there are any supernatural beings. Does that mean these Christian stories collapse or do they still work if we translate them into non-supernatural terms? Can these stories still inspire us without their supernatural guarantee?

I think the answer is yes. I think they are still alive. That is because I think humanity invented those supernatural beings in the first place. They were always part of our human capacity to apprehend the world in poetic terms. So what I want to do in this chapter is look at those three New Testament 'takes' on the Christian Grand Narrative and see what they say to us when translated into the language of common humanity, because I think we do need a Grand Narrative if we are not just to drift into futility or disaster. After that I will look at the theme of Incarnation, the theology of the Incarnate Word, starting from the great poem which is the prologue to John's Gospel.

The Kingdom of God

First the Grand Narrative of the coming of the reign of God. In Luke's Gospel when Jesus begins his ministry in Galilee, he goes into the synagogue and quotes the prophet Isaiah:

> The Spirit of the Lord is upon me
> because he has anointed me to bring good news to the poor.
> He has sent me to proclaim release to the captives
> and recovery of sight to the blind,
> to let the oppressed go free.[57]

The time has come, he says, the *kairos*, the right time. The time is *now*. In Luke, the Sermon on the Mount is the Sermon on the Plain and in fact the texts are *plainer*:

> Blessed are you who are poor, for yours is the kingdom of God.
> Blessed are you who are hungry now for you will be filled.[58]

Matthew's version adds:

> Blessed are the meek for they shall inherit the Earth.

Or perhaps we could translate it as: 'Blessed are the dispossessed for they shall have land.' And:

> Blessed are those who hunger and thirst for justice, for they shall be filled;
> Blessed are the peace makers.[59]

Jesus preaches the kingdom of God, a kingdom or reign of kindness – justice and peace – on Earth, which is good news for the poor and hungry. The world is turned upside down. The kingdom belongs *first and foremost* to the poor – the *anawim*, the 'losers'.[60] It is first and foremost for them *because*

---

[57] Lk 4: 18.
[58] Lk 6: 20.
[59] Mt 5: 5, 6.
[60] Terry Eagleton's translation in his *Reason, Faith, and Revolution: Reflections on the God Debate* (Yale University Press, 2009).

they are poor, not because they are nicer or better than other people. Like everyone else the *anawim* can be very annoying.

In preaching this kingdom Jesus reveals the God he believes in, whom he addresses intimately as 'Abba'. Jesus believed it was this God who guaranteed the rapid coming of the kingdom, already 'breaking in' with the good news he himself brought.

In his preaching Jesus acts freely and bravely. He is accompanied by both men and women. He chooses his followers freely, including the socially despised. As one of his disciples, he chooses the tax collector Levi.[61] He eats with whomever he pleases, with his friends, with Pharisees, and also with 'tax collectors and sinners', which causes scandal:

> And Levi made him a great feast in his house: and there was a large company of tax collectors and others sitting at table with them. And the Pharisees and their scribes murmured against his disciples saying: 'Why do you eat and drink with tax collectors and sinners?'[62]

Jesus acts freely with regard to the law and the Sabbath. He defends his disciples when the Pharisees attack them for failing to observe ritual handwashing before they eat: 'Don't you see that whatever goes into a man from outside cannot defile him, since it enters not his heart but his stomach and so passes on?'[63] When his disciples pluck a few ears of corn to eat as they pass through the cornfields on the Sabbath day and the Pharisees declare it is unlawful, Jesus replies: 'The Sabbath was made for man, not man for the Sabbath, so the son of man is

---

[61] Lk 5: 27; Mk 2: 13; Mt 9: 9 where Levi is called Matthew.
[62] Lk 5: 29.
[63] Mk 7: 18.

lord even of the Sabbath.'[64] He heals people on the Sabbath day, including a man with a withered hand. This so enrages the Pharisees that they 'went out and conspired against him, how to destroy him'.[65]

He is anti-authoritarian and anti-clerical, particularly when power and authority are abused. He 'insultingly denounces oppressors, those who offend little ones, who lead people astray, and he pays no heed to the consequences to himself that stem from this conduct.'[66] He attacks the Pharisees: 'You brood of vipers! How can you speak good when you are evil?'[67] The Pharisees 'bind heavy burdens, hard to bear... do all their deeds to be seen by men... love the place of honour at feasts and the best seats in the synagogues.' [68] He attacks the scribes who 'devour widows' houses and for the sake of appearances say long prayers'.[69] In the kingdom of God the greatest must 'become like children'[70] and whoever offends one of these little ones, 'it would be better for him to have a great millstone fastened round his neck and to be drowned in the depth of the sea'.

Jesus is certainly not 'intensely relaxed about the filthy rich'. He condemns them: 'Woe to you that are rich, for you have received your consolation.'[71] It is very hard for the rich to enter the kingdom. Bankers with big bonuses should beware: 'It is easier for a camel to go through the eye of a needle than

---

[64] Mk 2: 27–8; Mt 12: 1–8; Lk 6: 1–5.

[65] Mt 12: 14; Mk 3: 6.

[66] Jon Sobrino, *Jesus the Liberator,* translated by Paul Burns and Francis McDonagh (Orbis Books, New York 1993), p. 145. Abbreviated as *Jesus* in subsequent notes.

[67] Mt.12: 34.

[68] Mt 23: 4–6.

[69] Lk 20: 47.

[70] Mt 18: 3.

[71] Lk 6: 24.

for a rich man to enter the kingdom of God.'[72] As the disciples probably thought that wealth showed God's favour, 'they were greatly astounded and said to one another: "Then who can be saved?" '

When Jesus gets to Jerusalem:

> He entered the temple and began to drive out those who were selling and those who were buying in the temple, and he overturned the tables of the money-changers and the seats of those who sold doves.[73]

He told these merchants they had made the temple 'a den of thieves'. That was the last straw for the chief priests and the scribes. 'When the chief priests and the scribes heard of it, they kept looking for a way to kill him.'[74] 'Jesus' preaching and activity represented a radical threat to the religious power of his time, and indirectly to any oppressive power, and that power reacted.' [75]

Jesus was perfectly aware that in attacking the powerful, the religious authorities – chief priests, scribes and Pharisees – and the rich, he was setting himself on a collision course. He was convinced he would be killed. In a sense he 'asked for it'. His view of the kingdom, which was first and foremost for the poor and the 'little ones', indeed turned the world upside down. In going to his death he identified with these 'losers' and became one of them. He also thought his death would help bring in the kingdom, as God would vindicate him.[76] And as a matter of fact in history, any attempt to bring in 'the

---

[72] Mk 10: 25.
[73] Mk 11: 15.
[74] Mk 11: 18.
[75] *Jesus,* p. 196.
[76] Mt 17: 22; Mk 8: 31; Lk 9: 21.

kingdom' or a better society has involved confronting oppressors. As the liberation theologian, Jon Sobrino, puts it:

> Jesus knew and accepted the battle of the gods, and the negative power of history which puts prophets to death.

But:

> Let it be said from the start that the historical Jesus did not interpret his death in terms of salvation, in terms of the soteriological models later developed by the New Testament, such as expiatory sacrifice or vicarious satisfaction.[77]

The synoptic Gospels make clear:

> The final reality for Jesus was not himself, but neither was it the purely ahistorical transcendence suggested by 'kingdom of heaven', and of course it was not the church... not only did Jesus not preach himself, but the final reality for him was not simply 'God' but the 'kingdom of God'... for Jesus even God is seen within a wider reality of the 'kingdom of God'.[78]

Sobrino, quoted above, happened to be abroad and so survived when in November 1989 his whole Jesuit community at the University of Central America in San Salvador was murdered by the Salvadorean army Atlacatl Battalion. At that time the USA was funding the Salvadorean army $1m dollars per day and training its officers in 'counter-insurgency' techniques in the notorious School of the Americas.[79] The Atlacatl Battalion's motto is: 'For country and with God'.

---

[77] *Jesus*, p. 201.
[78] *Jesus*, p. 68.
[79] See Jon Sobrino, *Companions of Jesus: The Murder and Martyrdom of the Salvadorean Jesuits,* translated by Dinah Livingstone (CIIR, London 1989).

Sobrino has written a great deal about the 'kingdom' or 'reign' of God. He says: 'It is the reality of Latin America today and of the Third World in general that calls for a reign of God... The major fact in Latin America is the massive, unjust poverty that threatens whole populations with death. At the same time the most novel fact is the hope of a just life, of liberation.'[80] So: 'We have to announce God's kingdom in the presence of the anti-kingdom ruled by idols and in opposition to them.'[81] Idols are 'false gods that demand and feed on death' and the idol mentioned by name in the Sermon on the Mount is Mammon, worshipped today by an aggressive global capitalism.

The kingdom is both personal and political – within us and among us. It is personal because the individual has to *want* a reign of kindness, justice and peace in order to belong to it. It is no use just grabbing as much as ever you can and to hell with everyone else. The kingdom is political because it is about a good society. And in our globalised world the *polis* has to be the whole Earth – an end to poverty, hunger, misery, curable disease, an end to unjust wars. Jesus said the kingdom belongs first and foremost to the poor. That means that not only should the poor have the wherewithal to live a decent life but also that we who are rich, either as individuals or as a society, should at least *moderate* our demands, or we will be excluded from the kingdom. Or it will never come at all – our planet will die. The poor have a privileged position in the kingdom – they come first – because it is *not* a good society if they are excluded. In that sense the poor can save *us*. The kingdom is

---

[80] Jon Sobrino, 'Central Position of the Reign of God in Liberation Theology' in *Mysterium Liberationis: Fundamental Concepts of Liberation Theology*, ed. Ignacio Ellacuría and Jon Sobrino (Orbis Books, New York 1993), p. 356.

[81] Jon Sobrino, 'The Winds of Santo Domingo and the Evangelisation of Culture' in *Santo Domingo and After* (CIIR, London 1993), p. 30.

political because it is about co-operation or, 'love your neighbour as yourself' – *political* love.

We have seen the anti-kingdom at work, for example in the extraordinary campaigns of US health businesses and their allies to prevent the implementation of what they called 'Obama's Nazi Health Scheme' – his attempt to bring some sort of universal health care to the USA where over 46 million people can't afford any health insurance at all. The kingdom is political because the anti-kingdom, the pursuit of wealth or growth at all costs and at the expense of others, not only excludes the vast mass of humanity from a life fit for human beings, but also now threatens to destroy the Earth herself by over-exploitation.

Jesus says that he is inaugurating the kingdom but it is not yet complete. It is both *now* and *not yet*. At his Last Supper he says: 'I have eagerly desired to eat this Passover with you before I suffer: for I tell you I shall not eat it again until it is fulfilled in the kingdom of God.'[82] He thought the kingdom or reign was going to come quite soon. For example, he says: 'I tell you truly, there are some standing here who will not taste of death before they see the kingdom of God.'[83] He was wrong. As Sobrino comments:

> Jesus' ignorance is not of detail but affects something as central to him and as important in itself as when the kingdom is to come. The nucleus of these words appears to be historical and shows Jesus not merely not knowing but making a mistake; no one can answer this by saying that the kingdom had in fact come in Jesus, since even if what the

---

[82] Lk 22: 15.
[83] Lk 9: 27.

kingdom is was (later) interpreted in this sense, Jesus himself did not see it in this way.[84]

But of course people on Earth are still poor and hungry and we are still waiting for the reign of kindness, justice and peace on Earth. When Jesus went away and did not return, when that reign did not come on Earth within one generation, gradually the story of the kingdom was transferred to heaven above.

Jesus told many parables about the kingdom, such as the parables of the Sower and of the Wedding Feast. Jesus thought a supernatural God would guarantee the coming of this kingdom on Earth. Just as Jesus was wrong about when the kingdom would come, I think he was also mistaken in believing that a supernatural God exists and would bring in the kingdom. So what remains of his gospel? We can also regard this supernatural God story as a fiction, a parable: of the good ruler who appears in power and throws out the oppressors and vindicates the oppressed.

If we do not believe in a supernatural God, we have *no* guarantee of a happy ending to the story, but we can still believe in the 'gospel'. As we said in chapter 1, the original meaning of the English word 'believe', related to German *lieben,* is to cherish or hold dear. It is in that sense we can still believe in the gospel of the kingdom or reign of justice, peace and kindness on Earth: a vision of abundant lives, a happy humanity at home on a well-cared-for Earth, a global society in which everyone has a decent chance. Faith is 'the substance of things hoped for'. We can set our hearts on it. We can have faith that it *should* happen, that it *could* happen, even if we have no supernatural guarantee that it *will.* And even if it never happens completely, as it is an ideal of perfection, it is better

---

[84] *Jesus,* p. 153.

that it should happen a bit than not at all. We can have faith in it by taking its side. The kingdom is political but it is not a political programme. We have to work it out for ourselves, embody it in human lives and institutions. It is a humanist vision, the grandest of all Grand Narratives.

The Body of Christ

Another related way of describing the fulfilment of humanity was to see it as one single body growing to maturity. This image of all human beings as organically connected and interdependent is a powerful one.

Jesus gives a version of the whole of humanity as himself in his story (beginning with *food*) of the sheep and the goats. At the judgment of the nations, he says to those on his right hand:

> Come and inherit the kingdom prepared for you; for I was hungry and you gave me food. I was thirsty and you gave me drink, I was a stranger and you welcomed me, I was naked and you clothed me, I was sick and in prison and you visited me... Truly I tell you, as you did it to one of the least of these my brothers and sisters you did it to me.[85]

On the road to Damascus, Paul 'still breathing threats and murder' against the Christians, was floored by his vision of Jesus. What Jesus said to him was: 'Saul, Saul, why do you persecute *me*?'[86] Once again what is done to 'the least of these my brothers and sisters' is done 'to me', as Jesus identifies himself with his growing *body* of followers.

---

[85] Mt 25: 34.
[86] Acts 9: 4.

In his Letter to the Corinthians[87] Paul recalls that 'the Lord Jesus on the night when he was betrayed took bread... broke it and said: "This is my body..." ' That is what leads Paul to go on to reflect on the new humanity as one body: 'For just as the body is one and has many members, and all the members of the body, though many, are one body, so it is with Christ.'[88] Christ is the name for the new liberated humanity.

Paul's Letters are the earliest New Testament writings we have. In them and in those traditionally ascribed to him, such as Colossians and Ephesians,[89] we find the Christ Epic, which became attached to Jesus. Christ is both Jesus and the figurehead, the namesake hero of his people, the new Adam, representative of humanity in all its potential. Perhaps surprisingly, the Pauline Letters are full of poems. Christ's incarnation, death, descent to the lowest depths and resurrection becomes an epic story, poem or drama of humanity's – and the whole Earth's – struggle for liberation. I'll quote briefly from three of them.

In his Letter to the Philippians[90] Paul writes or quotes a poem, which may have been an early Christian hymn, focusing on the *shape* of the drama – Christ Jesus:

who, though he was in the form of God,
did not regard equality with God
as something to be exploited,
but emptied himself,
taking the form of a slave,
being born in human likeness.

---

[87]   1 Cor 11: 23.

[88]   1 Cor 12: 12.

[89]   Although some scholars think Colossians and Ephesians were written by Paul, others (more in the case of Ephesians) think they were probably written by a member of his 'school'.

[90]   Phil 2: 5.

And being found in human form,
he humbled himself
and became obedient to death –
even death on a cross.
Therefore God also highly exalted him
and gave him the name
that is above every name,
so that at the name of Jesus
every knee should bend
in heaven and on Earth and under the Earth.

In the Colossians poem[91] Christ is:

the image of the invisible god,
the firstborn of all creation;
for in him all things in heaven and on Earth were created,
things visible and invisible,
whether thrones or dominions or rulers or powers –
all things have been created through him and for him.
He himself is before all things,
and in him all things hold together.
He is the head of the body, the church;
he is the beginning, the firstborn from the dead,
so that he might come to have first place in everything.
For in him all the fullness of God was pleased to dwell.

Or in our third poem, Ephesians this time:[92]

When he ascended on high,
he led captivity captive
and gave gifts to humanity.
When it says 'He ascended',
what does it mean but that he had also descended
into the lowest parts of the Earth?
He who went down

---

91   Col 1: 15–19.
92   Eph 4: 7.

95

is the same one who went up
far above all the heavens
so that he might fill all things.

The movement is *down* and then *up* of Christ, one who was 'in the form of God', 'emptying himself' down to Earth, assuming humanity even in its lowest form, its most painful mortality, death on a Cross, and then this humanity *in Christ* being *highly exalted*.

This new humanity is seen as *collective*, an articulated body with Christ as its head and with different members playing the different, necessary roles: 'For if the whole body were an eye, where would the hearing be? If the whole body were a ear, where would be the sense of smell? If all were a single member, where would the body be? ... Now you are the body of Christ and individually members of it.'[93] 'For as in one body we have many members and not all the members have the same function, so we, who are many, are one body in Christ, and individually we are members of one another.'[94]

In Colossians Christ is 'the head of the body, the church'. In him, 'the whole fullness of deity dwells bodily and you have come to fullness in him'.[95] In Ephesians God's 'plan for the fullness of time' is to 'sum up all things in Christ, things in heaven and things on Earth'.[96] The Greek word translated as 'sum up' is 'ἀνακεφαλαιωσασθαι *(anakephalaiosasthai)*, which could also be translated as 'recapitulate', and is related to κεφαλη *(kephale)* meaning 'head'. Christ is 'head over all things for the church, which is his body, the fullness of him who fills

---

93 1 Cor 12: 17, 27.
94 Rom 12: 4–5.
95 Col 2: 9.
96 Eph 1: 10.

all in all... so that he might create in himself one new humanity.'[97]

The project is 'the building up of the body of Christ, until ... all of us come to maturity, to the measure of the stature of the fullness of Christ.'[98] It is not yet complete. Paul can say: 'I fill up what is lacking in the sufferings of Christ, for the sake of his body, the church.'[99] Here too we have the tension between *now* and *not yet*. The epic is the myth of a people – in this case humanity – as the body of Christ coming to *embody* the divine wisdom,[100] 'the whole fullness of God'.[101]

The metaphor of the body of Christ sees humanity as *social* and *interdependent*. It is the opposite of Margaret Thatcher's famous dictum: 'There is no such thing as society.'[102] On the contrary, as Paul puts it when he is talking about the Eucharist to the Corinthians: 'We who are many are one body, because we all share the same bread.'[103] But then he goes on to castigate them because:

> When you come together, it is not really to eat the Lord's supper. For when the time comes to eat, each of you goes ahead with your own supper, and one goes hungry and another becomes drunk... You show contempt for the church of God and humiliate those who have nothing.[104]

This idea of humanity as one *social* body reaching 'maturity', its full potential, is another take on the Grand Narrative of

---

kingdom come. At the moment humanity clearly does *not* all share the same bread. Some eat far too much and some starve.

Eating and drinking are an important theme in the gospels. Indeed Jesus' enemies criticise him as a 'gluttonous man and a wine bibber'. As we saw earlier, he eats with anyone he pleases, including 'tax collectors and sinners'. He works wonders with a few loaves, feeding five thousand people. The first criterion at the Judgment is: 'I was hungry and you gave me *food*.' At the Last Supper he says: 'I have eagerly desired to eat this Passover with you before I suffer; for I tell you, I will not eat it again until it is fulfilled in the kingdom of God. Then he took the cup…'[105] Several of the resurrection appearances involve eating, including the Eucharist at Emmaus. Jesus is 'the Lord of the shared table'. The fulfilment of humanity is represented as a feast, a 'Messianic banquet'.

However, once again there is something 'scandalous' here – offensive to the rich and powerful. Once again the gospel turns the world upside down. Just as people were scandalised that the kingdom belonged first and foremost to the poor and it was very hard for the rich to enter it, here the scandal is that Jesus was crucified, his body was *broken*:

> But we preach Christ *crucified,* a stumbling block to Jews and folly to Gentiles, but to those who are called, both Jews and Greeks, Christ the power of God and the wisdom of God.[106]

As Jon Sobrino puts it: 'Christ has a body that makes him present in history. So we need to ask whether this body is crucified.'[107] Sobrino then goes on to speak of all the poor, the

---

[105] Lk 22: 15.
[106] 1 Cor 1: 20.
[107] *Jesus,* p. 254.

hungry, the oppressed, the excluded, the *anawim* and calls them the 'crucified people' who are:

> the actual presence of the crucified Christ in history, as Archbishop Romero said to some terrorised peasants who had survived a massacre: 'You are the image of the pierced saviour.' ... the crucified people embody Christ in history as crucified. [108]

Like Jesus, they are crucified by the 'sin of the world', the 'structural sin' which is 'the ongoing negation of the reign of God':[109] the poverty and death inflicted on them by the power of the 'idols of death', including Mammon, worshipped today by an aggressive global capitalism. Jesus, executed as a criminal by the powers that ruled his world, identified with these sufferers. As Terry Eagleton puts it: Christ crucified is 'the ultimate signifier of the human condition'.[110]

We saw the gospel of the kingdom was both personal and political and the same is true of the metaphor of the body of Christ. It is personal because it requires us to behave kindly to our fellow human beings, as fellow members of one body. It is personal because, as it is the body of Christ, it invites us to remember Jesus, who asked us to: 'Do this in memory of me.'[111] But that Eucharist 'in memory of me' is not just an act of personal piety; it is a 'shared table'. The metaphor of the body of Christ has *social* and not only social but *political* connotations. Just as the kingdom does not come if the poor are excluded, so Christ is still crucified while so many continue to suffer unjustly and unnecessarily in our late capitalist world

---

[108] *Jesus*, p. 255.
[109] Jon Sobrino, 'Central Position of the Reign of God', p. 355.
[110] *Reason, Faith, and Revolution: Reflections on the God Debate.*
[111] Lk 22: 19.

today. Yet in their hope and their struggle these 'crucified people' are rising again.

The power of Christ's resurrection is the *vindication* of himself as 'the firstborn' and of all those other crucified people who are his suffering body in history. It embodies the hope that humanity may one day overcome unjust suffering and exploitation and become a 'glorified body'. And for this story to retain its power there is no need to believe that Jesus' corpse was literally resuscitated. Many highly respected theologians do not think that it was. For example, the Uruguayan Jesuit Juan Luis Segundo writes:

> Everything I have examined concerning the literary genre of the evangelical accounts of the resurrection shows us that, although these seem to contain the most sensational miracle in the story of Jesus, they do not, strictly speaking, relate any miracle at all. The presence of the eschatological comes about without the need to break or replace any natural law.[112]

Here there is no space to discuss this question, about which such an enormous amount has been written. We may just note that in the earliest written account we have in the New Testament of the resurrection appearances, the list given by Paul in his Letter to the Corinthians,[113] the word he repeatedly uses (four times in one paragraph) is 'ωφθη *(ophthe)*, an aorist *passive* form meaning 'he was seen'. Paul uses this same word for his own *vision* of Jesus on the road to Damascus as well as for all the other appearances.

---

[112] J.L. Segundo, *The Humanist Christology of Paul*, quoted in Jon Sobrino, *Christ the Liberator*, translated by Paul Burns (Orbis, New York 2001), p. 19.

[113] 1 Cor 15: 5.

Even for those of us who regard the whole supernatural realm as a product of the human imagination, this resurrection story retains its power. It embodies our experience of the countless ways in which life, vigour and joy can rise again in people who have been crushed or defeated. And above all, it embodies the hope that unjust suffering and oppression will not prevail forever, that humanity could finally get its act together and become a glorious body. We can read the whole Christ Epic as bringing the God whom *we* invented, *we* set in heaven, down to Earth, emptying himself back down into humanity and then that humanity aspiring back up to the ideals *we* set in God and coming to embody them. If we translate the epic into non-supernatural terms, as in the story of kingdom come, we have no guarantee that the happy ending will be reached. Once again, there is no problem in translating the image of humanity as a single body into a purely humanist vision. The difficulty is translating the vision into reality. With no God to ensure it, that is a purely human task.

Bridegroom and Bride

Now to the divine marriage. 'The Dark Night' is an extra-ordinary love poem by the Spanish mystic John of the Cross. In the poem the speaker and protagonist is a woman, who slips out unseen at night to meet her beloved and they are blissfully united. When they make love, she feels so at one with him that she might have become him, she could not have told herself from him. The poem works breathlessly well both as an account of mystical union with the divine and as a human love story. In the Spanish, the woman is called *amada*: 'beloved', feminine, and the man *amado*: 'beloved', masculine. The relationship is completely reciprocal. You can't tell who is loving and who is being loved. Both are doing both. She addresses the night:

O noche que juntaste:
    O night that joined [united]
amado con amada:
    beloved (m) with beloved (f)
amada en el amado transformada:
    beloved (f) changed into beloved (m)

This poem is famously difficult to translate because English does not have that grammatical felicity of a masculine and feminine past participle: you can't tell whether 'beloved' is male or female. It's a kind of Beecher's Brook for translators, a real challenge. Here is my attempt at this difficult verse. She exclaims to the night:

O night that guided,
O night more delightful than the dawn,
O night that united
beloved with beloved,
she who was his love changed into her love, him.

He lies asleep on her breast and she strokes his hair. The poem ends with her saying:

I stayed there and forgot myself,
I leant my face upon my beloved.
Everything stopped, I left myself,
all my care had faded
among the lilies forgotten.

John of the Cross was a mystic, who intended his poem to express union with the divine. Mystics of many cultures have often expressed that union in erotic terms. Some mystics believe their experience is supernatural and some do not. But the curious thing is, either way, what they describe is very similar. In his poem, although John believes his experience is supernatural, he has translated it into wonderful human poetry.

That blissful mystical union is the story of an individual spiritual journey. We saw with the Grand Narrative both of the kingdom of God and of the body of Christ that the message was both personal and political. We find the same is true here with this story of the divine marriage. For where have we heard those exclamations in praise of the night before? Where had the poet heard them before?

Surely in the *Exsultet*, the great praise poem for the paschal candle sung at the Easter Vigil with its repeated: '*Haec nox est*: 'This is the night... when you led our ancestors, the children of Israel, out of in Egypt to cross the Red Sea dry-shod...This the night when Christ broke the chains of death and ascended conqueror from hell ...' And: '*O vere beata nox*: O truly happy night... when heaven is married to Earth and God to humanity.' Later in the Easter Vigil the water is blessed in the font, and in what is surely a fertility ritual for a marriage night, the paschal candle is repeatedly plunged into it, with a prayer that the water may 'become fruitful'.

So we are back with the Christ Epic, but this time instead of the image of the whole Christ as a single body, we have the image of Christ the bridegroom with his bride, the united male and female human form divine. Jesus sometimes refers to himself as 'the bridegroom'.[114] Paul calls the church Christ's bride.[115] In Ephesians marriage is called 'a great mystery and I take it to mean Christ and the church.'[116] We find this image developed in the later book of Revelation. This is the wedding

---

[114] Mt 9: 15; Lk 5: 34.
[115] 2 Cor 11: 2.
[116] Eph 5: 32.

of the Lamb, and as we say, the wedding is the bride's day.
Now the bride is a beautiful city.

The Beautiful City

> I saw the holy city, the new Jerusalem, coming down out of
> heaven from God, as a bride prepared for her husband...
> And I heard a loud voice from the throne saying: 'See the
> dwelling of God is among humans.'[117]

God comes down to Earth He comes down into human
society – the city, the *polis* – which finally comes to embody
the qualities of kindness we set as ideals in God. That is a
humanist political vision, which is both now and not yet. It
inspired our London poet Blake in his great poem *Jerusalem*:

> The fields from Islington to Marybone,
> to Primrose Hill and St John's Wood,
> Were builded over with pillars of gold
> And there Jerusalem's pillars stood.
>
> Her little ones ran on the fields,
> The Lamb of God among them seen,
> And fair Jerusalem his Bride
> Among the little meadows green.
>
> Pancras and Kentish Town repose
> Among her golden pillars high,
> Among her golden arches which
> Shine upon the starry sky.

Of course, London can also be the city of dreadful night.
Camden Town tube station late at night is a horrible edgy
place with drug dealing and the threat of violence. But the idea

---

[117] Rev 21: 2.

of the new Jerusalem is the vision of a beautiful city, a good society. Walking about London you get visionary glimpses of it. From Parliament Hill, where kites are flying, you can look down on 'London flower of cities all' and people strolling on Hampstead Heath engage in countless conversations. London is a city of 300 languages. That is one description of a city: umpteen conversations. London is its people. They say love is builder of cities. On fine days on the Heath you see the young couples coming out to picnic, with their bag of goodies and bottle of wine. Work is also builder of cities. Londoners working. On the top deck of the bus a nurse going home in the dark after a long shift sits dozing and knitting. The bus driver knows her route. In the early morning I see the little group of building workers standing outside the caff with their fags and big polystyrene cups of tea. I go to my corner shop and the shopkeeper, who just happens to speak Bengali, Urdu, Hindi, English and a bit of Arabic, laughs when I can't resist buying yet more of his wonderfully cheap plants for my small garden. Or I can buy scented mangoes and any number of spices. He is a Muslim but at Christmas, he shoved a bottle of wine into my shopping bag as a seasonal gift.

In St Botolph's Without Aldgate, which stands just where the East End meets the city of London, as you enter the church the focal point behind the altar is a marvellous modern batik, which depicts the tree of life and the river of the water of life flowing through new Jerusalem, the twelve-gated city. Seen in the background, the transfigured golden city has a silhouette that could be London. Again the poetic image of the new Jerusalem is not a political programme but it can inspire the vision of a city, which must be worked out in practice. Mayor Ken Livingstone's best moments were inspired by his vision of London, the city he loves. I'd just like to quote from Ken's speech the day after the 7/7 London bombings, which was infused with his vision of London:

This was not a terrorist attack against the mighty and the powerful. It was not aimed at presidents or prime ministers. It was aimed at ordinary, working-class Londoners – black and white, Muslim and Christian, Hindu and Jew, young and old …

Then he said to the bombers:

In the days that follow look at our airports, look at our sea ports and look at our railway stations, and even after your cowardly attack, you will see that people from the rest of Britain, people from around the world will arrive in London to become Londoners and to fulfil their dreams and achieve their potential. They choose to come to London, as so many have come before, because they come to be free, they come to live the life they choose, they come to be able to be themselves.

Though Ken Livingstone did not use religious language, he was speaking out of the English radical tradition, which has strong Christian roots, deep in the Christian Grand Narrative. I've quoted him and spoken about London, my city, but of course our political vision must be global – act local think global. That is the vision of the New Jerusalem, the marriage of heaven and Earth. We don't have to take the supernatural bits literally. It is a story, a myth, an allegory, not difficult to translate into a purely human vision, but of course much more difficult to embody in the reality of our lives on Earth.

Jesus who announced the kingdom of God, the reign of justice and peace on Earth; the Christ Epic that was attached to him, the namesake hero of a new humanity as one body, all sharing the same bread; the bridegroom with his bride, the beautiful city the new Jerusalem: these three stories are a single Grand Narrative of a whole liberated, humane humanity at home on Earth. The Grand Narrative has been sneered at and dismissed because we no longer believe in its supernatural components. But talking in parables about the kingdom, or talking about humanity as a single body or a beautiful city and bride, are *already* poetic tropes, metaphor, allegory. We just have to figure that the supernatural elements – such as God – are *also* poetic tropes. Then it is not difficult to translate into purely human terms – losing the supernatural guarantee.

We need a Grand Narrative for the maturity of humanity, fulfilling its potential and being sane enough to look after the Earth. We can translate the one we've got already into our own common language. Of course, it must be a good translation *both* with the right resonances in our own culture with our major concerns today, *and* faithful to the gospel of human kindness flowering on Earth. Then the Grand Narrative is not dead. In the words of Great-Heart: 'I have often been through this valley and have been much harder put to it than now I am. Yet you see I am alive.'[118]

Incarnate Word

John, the last of the four gospels, begins with a poem:

> In the beginning was the Word
> and the Word was with God
> and the Word was God.
> He was in the beginning with God.
> All things were made through him
> and without him nothing was made that was made.
> In him was life
> and the life was the light of humanity.
> The light shines in the darkness
> and the darkness did not overcome it…

---

[118] John Bunyan, *The Pilgrim's Progress,* part 2.

He was in the world
and the world was made through him;
yet the world did not know him.
He came into his own,
and his own did not accept him…

And the Word was made flesh
and lived among us,
and we have seen his glory
the glory as of a father's only son,
full of grace and truth.

In John's Gospel Jesus claims to have existed before his earthly life 'from the beginning'. He tells the Jews: 'Before Abraham was, I am.'[119] In the Prologue quoted above, the usual translation of verse 1b – προς τον θεον *(pros ton theon)* – is the Word was 'with God'. Another possible translation of προς *(pros)* is 'towards' or 'to'. So we would have the Word was 'towards God'. That 'towards' could include a connotation of 'about' God.

What word? The first answer that springs to mind is 'I AM': YHWH, God's word for himself, his name for himself, which he told Moses from the burning bush. The name YHWH is a *verb*. It is probably an archaic form of the verb 'to be'. As well as I AM, it might mean I CAUSE TO BE (the Hebrew verb has a causative form), or I WILL BE.

As in the example of what he said about Abraham above, Jesus frequently claims this divine 'I AM' in John's Gospel. John's Prologue ends: 'No one has ever seen God. It is God the only Son, who is close to the Father's heart, who has made

---

[119] Jn 8: 58.

him known.'[120] As the familiar Christmas hymn puts it, he is 'Word *of* the Father, now in flesh appearing'.

The term *logos* (word) is used in Greek philosophy and also has roots in the Old Testament, where God's creative word (*dbhar*) is also his deed:

> By the word of the Lord the heavens were made
> and all their host by the breath of his mouth.[121]

In the later Old Testament wisdom literature, God's word is called his wisdom. In the book of Sirach, Wisdom speaks in the first person:

> I came forth from the mouth of the Most High
> and covered the Earth like a mist.
> I dwelt in the highest heavens,
> and my throne was in a pillar of cloud...[122]

It was because I wanted to keep this reference to 'wisdom' as well as to 'word' that I risked subtitling this book *Logosofia Down to Earth*, despite the fact that, as I said in the Introduction, the word *logosofia* seems to have been invented by Coleridge and is not biblical. However, Christ *is* called both God's Word, as in John's Gospel, and God's Wisdom, as in Paul's Letter to the Corinthians.[123] 'Down to Earth' is taken from the Statement of Nicea quoted below, where Christ is said to have 'come down, become flesh, become human': κατελθοντα, σαρκωθεντα, 'ενανθρωπησαντα *(katelthonta,*

---

[120] Jn 1: 18
[121] Ps 33: 6.
[122] Sir 24: 3.
[123] 1 Cor 1: 24.

sarkothenta, enanthropesanta).[124] But I thought one Greek word in my subtitle was enough.

Beginning from the New Testament, the theology of Christ's humanity and divinity was worked out in fierce fights, with contenders taking a wide range of subtly different positions, some stressing his humanity and some his divinity. There is no space here to tell the story of those terrific battles. We can just recall briefly three important moments.

In 325 the Emperor Constantine called the first Ecumenical Council of Nicea to resolve the dispute between the followers of Athanasius and the followers of Arius. Arius thought that Jesus as a suffering human being *cannot* be God, but that he is the most exalted of all creatures, '*similar* in being' [of similar substance], ὁμοιουσιος *(homoíousios)*, to God. Athanasius, whose view prevailed, regarded Christ as fully divine and 'one in being' [of the same substance as], ὁμοουσιος *(homoousios, consubstantialis* in Latin), with God the Father. As Gibbon jeered, the difference between the two terms is just one iota – but enormous. Athanasius' term was adopted in the Statement of Nicea, which became the Nicene Creed:[125]

> We believe in … one Lord Jesus Christ, the son of God, born only-begotten of the Father, that is from the being of the Father, God of God, light of light, true God of true God, begotten not made, one in being[126] with the Father, through whom all things were made, those in heaven and those on

---

[124] These are aorist accusative participles agreeing with 'Jesus Christ' in the sentence beginning 'We believe in … one Lord Jesus Christ … come down, become flesh, become human.'

[125] Denzinger, *Enchiridion Symbolorum*, 31st edition, ed. Karl Rahner (Herder, Barcelona, Freiburg, Rome 1960), p. 29.

[126] ὁμοουσιον τω, πατρι *(homoousion to patri)*; Latin: *unius substantiae.*

Earth, who for us humans and our salvation came down,
became flesh, became human.

The Council of Ephesus in 431 reaffirmed the Nicene
Statement and further declared that Christ, fully divine and
fully human, was one *hypostasis* or person. Therefore it was
proper to call his mother Mary θεοτοκος *(theotokos),* meaning
'God-bearer': mother of God. A climactic third moment was
reached at the Council of Chalcedon in 451:[127]

> In agreement, therefore with the holy fathers,
> we all unanimously teach
> that we should confess our Lord Jesus Christ
> to be one and **the same**[128] Son,
> **the same** perfect in deity,
> and **the same** perfect in humanity,
> true God and true man,
> **the same** of a rational soul and body,
> one in being[129] with the Father in deity,
> **the same** one in being[130] with us in humanity,
> like us in all things except sin;
> begotten from the Father before the ages in deity,
> and in latter days, **the same,** for us and for our salvation,
> from the Virgin Mary mother of God in humanity:
> one and **the same** only-begotten Christ Son Lord,
> to be acknowledged in two natures
> without confusion, without change,
> without division, without separation,
> the difference of the natures
> being in no way removed because of the union,

---

[127] Denzinger p. 70.

[128] τον 'αυτον *(ton auton)*; Latin: *eundem.* This is the Greek and Latin for 'the
same' every time it is written in bold in the above quotation.

[129] 'ομοουσιον *(homoousion)*; Latin: *consubstantialem.*

[130] 'ομοουσιον *(homoousion)*; Latin: *consubstantialem.* The same term is used to
express Christ's full humanity as for his full divinity; he is wholly
human as well as wholly divine.

but with each nature's property remaining,
and running together into one person[131]
and one subsistence,[132]
not split or divided into two persons,
but one and **the same** Son and only begotten God
Word Lord Jesus Christ.

If we listen to the Chalcedon statement as a kind of poem, we hear how it stresses again and again that Christ, despite having both a human and a divine 'nature', is *the same* person. Listening to it aloud, you can't fail to hear the thunderous repetition of 'the same', 'the same', 'the same' (the repeated *eundem* in the Latin and τον 'αυτον – *ton auton* – in the Greek sound even more thunderous). The reason Mary is called 'mother of God' – θεοτοκος *(theotokos)* – is because you are not the mother of a 'nature' but a person. Although her Son Christ is said to have 'two natures', he is one and the *same* person. Another thing 'the thunder said' to me was this. Although the old church fathers who wrote the Chalcedon statement believed that God, including God the Son, existed 'before the ages' – eternally and independently of us – nevertheless that thunderous repetition conveys very powerfully that God and human are the same, the same, the same. Christ, who is both God and human, is *the same person*. Not only can a poem tell us things we didn't know we knew, but a whole poem can say more than its component parts.

Theologians like Augustine (354–430) struggled with the problem of how Christ the Word could be 'one in being' with the Father and yet not *be* the Father:

The Word of God, then, the only begotten Son of the Father, in all things like and equal to the Father, God of God, Light

---

[131] προσωπον *(prosopon)*; Latin: *personam.*
[132] 'υποστασιν *(hupostasin)*; Latin: *subsistentiam.*

of Light, Wisdom of Wisdom, Being of Being, is altogether that which the Father is, yet is not the Father, because the one is Son, the other is Father… As though uttering himself, the Father begot the Word equal to himself in all things; for he would not have uttered himself wholly and perfectly, if there were in his Word anything more or less than himself.[133]

The Word, which expresses God the Father's self-knowledge, is so perfect that it is a distinct person: the Son. And it is this wholly divine Son who has 'come down, become flesh, become human'.

One further thought about the θεοτοκος *(theotokos)*, a thought which may *not* have occurred to those old church fathers, is this. We notice that the Father and the Son are both masculine (and so, usually, is the Holy Spirit, about whom more in the next chapter). In ordinary life we think it sad for a son to be motherless and hard for a father without a female companion to cope with a child. The lone father–son relationship is idealised somewhat schmalzily by a novelist like Tony Parsons or in the hunky camaraderie of a Hollywood movie: 'Son, there comes a time in a man's life when a man's got to do what a man's got to do', which can sound hilarious. But usually a world without any feminine presence is *not* what we would regard as ideal. When the Son becomes human, he gains a mother and a bride (at least 'fair Jerusalem his bride'). We don't know whether Jesus actually had a wife or any lovers, but he certainly had women friends.

Chalcedon states that Christ the Word continues to be fully divine when he becomes human and also that he is fully and completely human, with a body and soul (as against those who thought the Logos merely 'inhabited' a human body). Because the human and divine Christ is one person, not only can Mary

---

[133] Augustine, *De Trinitate*, Bk 15: 14: 23.

be called 'mother of God' but whatever can be said about the man Jesus can be said of God (technically, this is called the *communicatio idiomatum*: 'sharing of properties'), so it can be said that God was born, God suffered, God died on the cross…

Earlier, we saw that there was something *scandalous* about Jesus' preaching of the kingdom of God,[134] the fact that the kingdom belonged first and foremost to the poor; and something scandalous about the body of Christ, that his body was *broken*. Paul preached 'Christ crucified'. In the theological process that culminated in the Statement of Chalcedon, what was 'a scandal to the Jews and mere foolishness to the Greeks' was this 'sharing of properties': being able to say God *suffered*.

'One and **the same** Son and only begotten God Word Lord Jesus Christ' is 'to be acknowledged in two natures without confusion, without change, without division, without separation, the difference of the natures being in no way removed because of the union, but with each nature's property remaining, and running together into one person…' Chalcedon holds the tension, the 'both-and'. It states the paradox as strongly as possible but does not resolve it. It uses philosophical terms like *homoousios*, which *state* but do not *explain* anything. I think the only thing we can do is read it as a poem. As Wittgenstein said, *'Philosophie dürfte man eigentlich nur dichten:* Actually philosophy should be just making poetry', or more loosely: 'The only way to do philosophy is to make it poetry'.

It is a poem of *humanity*. The whole creation by the human poetic genius of the supernatural and divine is brought within the *scope* of humanity, brought *down to Earth*. It has 'come

---

134 The kingdom of God and any *history* of what Jesus said and did, apart from his birth, death and resurrection, are absent from the Chalcedon statement. We will say more about that in the next chapter.

down, become flesh, become human'. Christ is *salus quoniam caro*. The salvation he brings comes through his humanity, 'even to death, death on a cross'. And we notice that Chalcedon's strongest possible assertion of Christ as *both* human *and* divine produces the most humanist outcome. The *whole fullness of God* is 'recapitulated' in a human being, who represents the whole human race. In his poem *Jerusalem*, Blake speaks of Jesus as 'the Lord, the Universal Humanity'. Theologians such as Teilhard de Chardin and Matthew Fox speak about the 'cosmic Christ'. The 'whole Christ' is an epic poem, the *poiesis* (making) of humanity.

Becoming human in Christ, God becomes Incarnate Word, which is a poem, a *poiesis* (making) of humanity in all its potential. It is also a poem, a vision of humanity 'in the making' – a prophetic poem. There is no supernatural guarantee that the prophecy will come to pass.

And because Christ the person is both God and man we can say that, as divine and human Word, he is also a poem, *poiesis* (making) *of God,* whose name is not only 'I AM' but 'I WILL BE'. In chapter 1 we saw the association of the German words *dichten* = 'to make a poem' and *dicht* = 'thick'. We could say that in the human Christ, God is *gedichtet* i.e. 'poemed', expressed as a poem, with the 'thickness' of human flesh and blood. The theology of the Incarnation, beginning in the New Testament and reaching a peak at the Council of Chalcedon, with its reiterated mantra, *the same, the same, the same,* brings God *down* into humanity.

In human beings, Anthony Freeman[135] has suggested that just as consciousness is an 'emergent property' of the brain, 'God' is an emergent property of human consciousness. In

---

[135] In 'Open up to God', *Sofia* 82, March 2007.

other words, we create and to some extent become 'God' as our consciousness expands. Of course, human beings (as individuals or as a species) can never attain infinite knowledge, but throughout our lives we can go on becoming more conscious. God, Freeman suggests, 'is altogether best understood as a high-level emergent property'. So we are back with Coleridge and his *Logosofia*: 'Therefore the human race… approach to and might become one body whose head is Christ (the Logos).' Or as Athanasius put it, speaking of the Word of God: 'He became human so that we might become God.' [136]

But a high level of consciousness is not enough. As Paul says: 'If I understand all mysteries and all knowledge… but do not have love, I am nothing.'[137] The next and final chapter is about love and kindness.

---

[136] Athanasius, *On the Incarnation,* 54.
[137] 1 Cor 13: 2.

Chapter 4

Human Kindness

The Spirit of Kindness

What kind of creatures are humans? We noted one paradox about us in chapter 1: that we are poetic animals. Another paradox is that we are the only animals who can be unkind. A cat that plays with a mouse is not being unkind; it is acting by instinct. We have a choice. So what do we mean by kind? We call our species humankind and if we describe it we have to say that it is capable of great generosity and great cruelty; it can attain amazing knowledge and be extremely foolish. But if we say that humankind *ought* to be kind to one another, we mean warm-hearted, friendly and loving, and we call that *humanity*. Kindness and humanity are *fellow feeling*. We can speak of a spirit of kindness, a spirit of humanity, which is a way of feeling and, above all, behaving towards one another.

In the last chapter we considered Christ as Incarnate Word and 'word' has to do with knowing and speaking. During the early Christian period there were Gnostic sects who thought that salvation comes purely through knowledge, being initiated into certain 'mysteries'. Paul, we saw, firmly rejects this: 'If I understand all mysteries and all knowledge… but do not have love, I am nothing.' Knowledge is not enough, wisdom is not enough, poetry is not enough. In fact, poets are famed for their feuding and religious people can be even more horrible, warring on each other, burning each other alive and so on. I remember the shock and disappointment I felt after reading St Bernard's wonderful works on the *Love of God* and the *Song of Songs* to discover how absolutely vile he was to Abelard at the

Council of Sens. And I expect we can all think of examples closer to home.

So what is this spirit of kindness? In the New Testament we hear about a mysterious 'spirit', which sometimes sounds like a distinct person and sometimes it is not clear. In the Greek New Testament the word is not spelt with an initial capital letter and in translations the capitalisation of the word varies considerably. In the quotations given below, the word 'spirit' is sometimes capitalised and sometimes not, and of course these choices can be questioned.

Like the Latin word *spiritus* (cf. 'respiration'), the Greek word for 'spirit', πνευμα *(pneuma)*, is related to 'breath'. The Greek πνευμα *(pneuma)* is neuter and although the Holy Spirit is translated as 'he' in the New Testament, there are some passages where this spirit occurs and could equally well be referred to as 'it'. To give just three examples:

> The spirit gives life; the flesh counts for nothing.[138]

> For if you live according to the flesh, you will die; but if by the spirit you put to death the deeds of the body, you will live. For all who are led by the spirit of God are sons of God. For you did not receive the spirit of slavery to fall back into fear, but you have received the spirit of sonship.[139]

> I know that through your prayers and the help of the spirit of Jesus Christ this will result in my deliverance.[140]

Here 'spirit' sounds rather like the 'spirit of London'.

---

[138] Jn 6: 63.
[139] Rom 8: 13–15.
[140] Phil 1: 19.

But sometimes the Spirit sounds more like a distinct person, or indeed, like a distinct person equal to the Father and the Son, as in the triple formulae at the end of 2 Corinthians: 'The grace of the Lord Jesus Christ, the love of God and the communion of the Holy Spirit be with all of you';[141] and at the end of Matthew's Gospel: baptising 'in the name of the Father and of the Son and of the Holy Spirit'. [142] The reader can assess how personal or impersonal this spirit is in the passages quoted below. In art the Father and the Son are often represented in human form but the Holy Spirit is likely to be a dove or even just tongues of fire or wind. So perhaps it was this 'spirit' that led the way towards desupernaturalisation, towards a non-supernatural spirit of kindness, of humanity.

Before Paul's great hymn to love in his Letter to the Corinthians, he has said to them: 'For in the one spirit we were all baptised into one body – Jews or Greeks, slaves or free – and we were all made to drink of one spirit.' He then goes on to describe all the different gifts and abilities various members of the body may have and concludes: 'But strive for the greater gifts. And I will show you a more excellent way.'[143] Love is the greatest gift of the spirit. Paul's praise of love continues:

> Love is patient; love is kind; love is not envious or boastful or arrogant or rude, it does not insist on its own way, it is not irritable or resentful; it does not rejoice in wrongdoing but rejoices in the truth. It bears all things, believes all things, hopes all things, endures all things. Love never ends.[144]

---

[141] 2 Cor 13: 13.
[142] Mt 28: 19.
[143] 1 Cor 12: 31.
[144] 1 Cor 13: 4–8.

This more or less personal spirit, whose greatest gift is love, occurs regularly in Paul's Letters. Just a few examples. Paul tells the Galatians that they are now God's children and 'God has sent the spirit of his Son into our hearts crying "Abba! Father!" '[145] To the Romans he speaks of 'the spirit of him who raised Jesus from the dead',[146] and goes on to say: 'For all who are led by the spirit of God are children of God... When we cry "Abba! Father!" it is that very Spirit bearing witness with our spirit that we are children of God.' In his Letter to the Philippians, as well as 'the spirit of Jesus Christ',[147] he speaks of 'the spirit of God'.[148] The Spirit is of both the Father and the Son.

This is the Holy Spirit who descended upon Jesus in the form of a dove when he was baptised;[149] who led Jesus into the wilderness to be tempted by the devil;[150] in whom Jesus 'rejoiced' and thanked his Father for having 'hidden these things from the wise and revealed them to infants'.[151] On the day of Pentecost after Jesus has left them, the Holy Spirit descends like a rushing mighty wind on the disciples huddled in the upper room, and rests on each of them like a tongue of fire.[152] After Paul's conversion vision on the road to Damascus, he is blinded until Ananias, a Christian living in Damascus, is sent to him and says: 'Brother Saul, the Lord Jesus, who appeared to you on your way here, has sent me so that you may regain your sight and be filled with the Holy Spirit.'[153]

---

[145] Gal 4: 6.
[146] Rom 8: 11.
[147] Phil 1: 19.
[148] Phil 3: 3.
[149] Lk 3: 22.
[150] Lk 4: 1.
[151] Lk 10: 21.
[152] Acts 2.
[153] Acts 9: 17.

In John's Gospel, Jesus tells Nicodemus: 'No one can enter the kingdom of God without being born of water and the spirit.'[154] Jesus invites all who are thirsty to come to him and drink and 'out of the believer's heart shall flow rivers of living water'. The evangelist comments: 'Now he said this about the Spirit, which believers in him were to receive: for as yet the Spirit had not been given, because Jesus was not yet glorified.'[155] In the long discourse, which John's Gospel sets just before Jesus goes out to his arrest and death, Jesus repeatedly tells his disciples to love one another and he promises them 'another Comforter': 'the Holy Spirit whom the Father will send in my name'.[156] Later he speaks of the Comforter, 'whom I will send to you from the Father, the Spirit of truth.'[157] The Spirit is sent either by the Father or the Son. For, Jesus says, 'All that the Father has is mine.'[158] Jesus concludes: 'It is to your advantage that I go away, for if I do not go away, the Comforter will not come to you; but if I go I will send him to you.'[159] The Spirit will not only help them understand, but is closely associated with loving one another.

In the First Letter of John, probably written by a member of the Johannine 'school', the stress is once again on love, the commandment, which is both old and new, to love one another. 'Whoever loves a brother lives in the light.'[160] 'We know that we have passed from death to life because we love one another. Whoever does not love abides in death.'[161] Once again love is associated with the Spirit: 'And this is his

---

[154] Jn 3: 5.
[155] Jn 7: 37–9.
[156] Jn 14: 26.
[157] Jn 15: 26.
[158] Jn 16: 15.
[159] Jn 16: 7.
[160] 1 Jn 2: 10.
[161] 1 Jn 3: 14.

commandment, that we should love one another... And by this we know that he abides in us by the Spirit that he has given us.'[162] Even more boldly the writer goes on to assert: 'God is love':

> Beloved, let us love one another, because love is from God; everyone who loves is born of God and knows God. Whoever does not love does not know God, for God is love... if we love one another, God lives in us, and his love is perfected in us. By this we know that we abide in him and he in us, because he has given us of his Spirit. ... God is love, and those who abide in love abide in God, and God abides in them.[163]

In our quest we may create all sorts of gods, but placating or pleasing these gods is not always an ethical or moral activity. The gods are not necessarily good, just powerful – they may personify powerful, real natural forces and you don't want to get on the wrong side of them. It's only when the will of God (or God himself) is equated with love (or goodness) that obeying him becomes an ethical activity. If God is love personified, or as Julian of Norwich says, 'love is his meaning', you obey his commandments by doing what love requires, by loving. But you could also do what love requires, you could also love, without personifying it. As Stevie Smith puts it in her poem about Jesus, 'Was he Married?':

> To choose a god of love, as he did and does,
> Is a little move then?
> Yes, it is.

But love is of supreme value whether or not we regard it as a supernatural person. As her poem continues, we can also 'love

---

love and hate hate' and 'not deify them'. In chapter 3 we described three New Testament ways of expressing the Christian Grand Narrative: the kingdom of God, the body of Christ, and the divine marriage. 'Love one another' is another way of putting it, summing up all three.

Spirit and Trinity

Christian monotheism worships one God but has also evolved the theology of the Trinity – Father, Son and Holy Spirit, three persons in one God. Curiously, these three persons are all usually regarded as male. There is a tradition, particularly in the East, of the Holy Spirit as female. It is echoed, for example, in Ernesto Cardenal's poem *The Music of the Spheres,* where he speaks of the Holy Spirit as *'espíritu o espírita'.* The normal Spanish word for 'spirit' is *el espíritu,* masculine. Cardenal invents the feminine term *espírita* to suggest that one could think of the Holy Spirit as feminine. But that tradition never became the dominant one.

As we have seen, the Spirit is mysterious in the New Testament and the theology of the Spirit developed more slowly than that of Father and Son. It was not until the Council of Constantinople in 381 that the Spirit was formally declared co-equal with the Father and Son in the Holy Trinity. At the beginning of the fifth century Augustine records and explores this teaching in his *De Trinitate.* Very briefly, Augustine says that all three persons of the Trinity wholly possess the one same divine being or substance, everything that God is. They are one God but as three persons, they are distinguished by their *subsistent relationships.* The Father *begets* the Son and together they *breathe* the Holy Spirit. Just as the Word, which expresses God the Father's self-knowledge, is so perfect that it is a distinct person: the Son, so the Father and the Son love each other so perfectly that this love is also a distinct person, who proceeds from both of them, from their mutual love:

> The Holy Spirit, according to the Holy Scriptures is neither of the Father alone, nor of the Son alone, but of both; and so intimates to us the mutual love wherewith the Father and the Son reciprocally love one another: *communem qua invicem se diligunt pater et filius nobis insinuat caritatem.*[164]

In his *Summa Theologica* Thomas Aquinas develops his theology of the Trinity, closely following Augustine. He investigates why the Holy Spirit proceeds from *both* the Father and the Son:[165]

> From the fact that the Father and the Son mutually love one another it necessarily follows that this mutual love, the Holy Spirit, proceeds from both.

He quotes Augustine:

> 'The Holy Spirit is he whereby the Begotten is loved by the one begetting and loves his Begetter.'[166]

He concludes:

> As therefore we say that a tree flowers by its flower, so do we say that the Father, by the Word or the Son, speaks himself, and his creatures; and that the Father and the Son love each other and us, by the Holy Spirit of Love proceeding.[167]

Both Augustine and Thomas Aquinas go to great lengths to expound this very complex doctrine. With scholastic subtlety

---

[164] *De Trin.* Bk 15: 17: 27.
[165] *Summa* I: 37: 1.
[166] *De Trin.* Bk 6: 5: 7.
[167] *Summa* I: 37: 2.

Thomas expounds what is meant by the term 'person'. Incidentally, although Thomas insists that the Holy Spirit is a person, as we noted above, his 'personality' is still less fully 'realised' than that of the Father and the Son.

With his usual psychological insight, Augustine spends several books of *De Trinitate* investigating the human mind as the image of the Trinity:

> And this question we are endeavouring in some way to investigate in the human mind, in order that from a lower image, in which our own nature itself as it were answers, upon being questioned, in a way more familiar to ourselves, we may be able to direct a more practised mental vision from the enlightened creature to the unchangeable light.[168]

As Meister Eckhardt was to put it later: 'All the names we give to God come from an understanding of ourselves.'[169] Augustine explores the mind's three activities, memory, understanding and will, as distinct activities but as products of a single mind:

> Since, then, these three: memory, understanding, will, are not three lives, but one life; nor three minds, but one mind; it follows certainly that neither are they three substances, but one substance.[170]

Augustine thinks of the human mind as the image of the Trinity, but we can look at it the other way round – another Other Way Round insight. The Trinity is an ideal model of the possibilities of the human psyche. God the Father personifies the life, energy, that we receive from parents and from the

---

[168] *De Trin.* Bk 9: 12: 17.
[169] Quoted by Matthew Fox in *A New Reformation* (Inner Traditions, Rochester, USA, 2006), p. 62 in thesis no. 5 of his new 95 Theses.
[170] *De Trin.* Bk 10: 11: 18.

cosmos through evolution. By knowing himself he pours all this into his Son, his Word, with nothing held back, his whole divine nature, so that the Son has everything that the Father has. Then together they pour that same whole divine nature into the Spirit, into *love*, so that the Spirit is the personified 'mutual love with which they love one another'. The term used is 'circumincession' – 'flowing round into': being flows into speaking; being and speaking flow into loving; and speaking and loving flow back round into being. Similarly, although of course we are neither perfect nor infinite, we humans pour our energies into knowing and knowing how to. But knowing on its own is not enough for full humanity; loving is also necessary. On that Trinitarian model all our knowing should pour into loving. Or as Augustine and Thomas would put it, *breathe* love.

Another insight the theology of the Trinity brings to the human person is that God is *social* – three persons, reminding us that we ourselves need other people in order fully to become persons, to become human. As Thomas Berry puts it:[171]

> The loss of relationship, with its consequent alienation, is a kind of supreme evil in the universe. In the religious world this loss was traditionally understood as an ultimate mystery. To be locked up in a private world, to be cut off from intimacy with other beings, to be incapable of entering the joy of mutual presence – such conditions were taken as the essence of damnation.

---

[171] Brian Swimme and Thomas Berry, *The Universe Story* (HarperOne, New York 1992), p. 78. This view is also central to the interpretation of the Trinity by Brazilian theologian Leonardo Boff in *Trinity and Society* (Orbis Books, Maryknoll, NY 1988).

As well as seeing the Trinity as a model of the human psyche, we can look at it cosmically. 'Geologian' Thomas Berry describes a cosmic, material trinity and, as he was a Catholic priest, perhaps unsurprisingly it lies in the Augustinian/ Thomist tradition. In his major work (with mathematical cosmologist Brian Swimme), *The Universe Story,* Berry describes the triple Cosmogenetic Principle, which operates throughout the cosmos, and 'assumes that the dynamics of evolution are the same at every point in the universe'.[172] The Cosmogenetic Principle, he says, 'states that the evolution of the universe will be characterised by *differentiation, autopoiesis* and *communion* throughout time and space and at every level of reality'.

Of *differentiation* he says: 'The universe began in a con-centration of energy and at each instant has re-created itself new. The seemingly infinite power for transfiguration in every region of the universe speaks of an inexhaustible fecundity at the root of reality.'

Of *autopoiesis* (self-making) he says: 'From autocatalytic chemicals to cells, from living bodies to galaxies, we find a universe filled with structures exhibiting self-organising dynamics.'

And of *communion* he says: 'To be is to be related, for relationship is the essence of existence. In the very first instant when the primitive particles rushed forth, every one of them was connected to every other one in the entire universe.'[173]

With the evolution of animals these three constants of the Cosmogenetic Principle develop into mutation, niche creation and natural selection. Mutation is an illustration of differentiation; conscious choice or niche creation is a

---

[172] *Universe,* p. 66.
[173] *Universe,* pp. 74–7.

biological illustration of *autopoiesis* – the animal must find (or choose) a niche where it can adapt and flourish; and natural selection is the dynamism of communion: 'fit into the community and become a fully functioning participant or else you will be left out for good.'[174] And of course with the evolution of human beings, these three shaping powers become differentiation as the unique individual, the person; self-making as self-expression, enormously enhanced by language; communion as fellowship and love.

So here we have a Trinity that operates from the primal flaring forth of the universe. Berry and Swimme insist the Cosmogenetic Principle has been formulated by observing the universe: 'It is not something to be proven. It is a fundamental assumption based on the evidence we have of the universe's development.'[175] It is easy to see a parallel between that secular trinity and the theology of God as Trinity: God the Father as inexhaustible creative energy; God the Son as self-expression, Word; God the Holy Spirit as Love.

This is not to say that there is any supernatural principle at work in the universe. On the contrary, the contemplation of the universe may lead people to express reverence for it by *deifying* forces they find in it. The universe is real but, as we said, supernaturalisation is a poetic trope akin to personification and metaphor. When the human poetic genius created one God as Trinity, perhaps it did have 'enlarged and numerous senses' in its apprehension of the cosmos with its triple Cosmogenetic Principle. It is delightful to find the poetic tale of the divine Trinity echoed in the actual structure of the universe, as scientists are increasingly discovering it. Our praise is due to the majesty of the universe itself and the

---

174 *Universe*, p. 133.
175 *Universe*, p. 67.

beauty of the Earth, and we may well summon all the poetic craft at our command to do so.

The well-known beautiful last line of Dante's *Divine Comedy* is 'Love that moves the sun and the other stars.' Even when we know that the cosmic energy which created the sun and stars is not a loving supernatural being – that is a poetic trope – we can still appreciate the force of it. We look at the universe and 'see that it is good', marvelling that the *same* cosmic energy, via the *same* Cosmogenetic Principle, evolved into human beings, who *are* capable of loving. As Thomas Aquinas puts it, love operates 'by way of impulse and movement towards an object'.[176] Or Augustine, who describes in his *Confessions* how he had gravitated towards 'a cauldron of filthy loves'[177] before turning to God, says: 'My love is my weight'.[178]

To end this section on a more modest scale, readers who have come so far will probably have noticed that this book, after its initial chapter on the necessity of poetry, also has a trinitarian structure mirroring the Father, Son and Spirit – with chapter 2 on 'Mother and Father', chapter 3: 'Earthchild', and this final chapter 4 on the spirit of kindness.

Kind and Unkind

In the last chapter we looked at Jesus' preaching of the kingdom of God and the Christ Epic as ways of envisaging human fulfilment, humankind that has achieved its potential for a fully humane humanity. In this chapter we have been considering human kindness. But how far have we got and

---

[176] *Summa* I: 27: 4. Dante (1265–1321) and Thomas Aquinas (c. 1225–74) were both Italian and near contemporaries.
[177] *Confessions* III: 1: 1.
[178] *Confessions* XIII: 8: 9.

how much has Christianity contributed to this? We find a battle still going on between the kind and unkind, both within Christianity itself and in humanity at large.

Sobrino points out that there is no mention at all of the kingdom of God in the christological statements of the early church councils. The *history* of Jesus is neglected to concentrate on his *person*. He quotes Origen who calls Christ 'αυτοβασιλεια του θεου *(autobasileia tou theou):* 'the kingdom of God in person'. That led to a neglect of the gospel as 'good news for the poor' *on Earth* and focused more on Christ as a divine being now in heaven. The theology of Christ as human and divine, and humanity as the body of Christ, does not *necessarily* lead to a neglect of Jesus' own teaching about a just society, which is good news for the poor, but may do so if Jesus becomes a heavenly king, not grounded in human beings living on Earth. This de-earthing of the gospel coincided with Christianity's increasing respectability in the Roman Empire. It was the Emperor Constantine who convoked the Council of Nicea and when Christianity became the official religion of the Roman Empire it ceased 'to be counter-cultural when it needed to be... and the church was able, inhumanly, in the name of faith, to wipe out heretics and pagans, and to turn itself into the church of Christendom.'[179]

That church is *not* the kingdom of God, though it may pass itself off as such. It has even used its authority in league with the 'anti-kingdom' and, of course, has accumulated great wealth. Up to this day Christianity has often been cruel and harmful but has also produced saints and seers, who have striven for the gospel of the kingdom. Christian language has been used by both sides in the struggle for humanity. There is no space here to look back over that two-thousand-year

---

[179] Jon Sobrino, *Christ the Liberator,* p. 254.

history. In passing, we may just look at a couple of examples where Christian language inspired a struggle for justice.

Together with Wat Tyler, the hedge priest John Ball was one of the leaders of the Peasants' Revolt in 1381. Their slogan was: 'When Adam delved and Eve span, who was then the gentleman?' Ball argued that 'things cannot go well in England, nor ever shall, till everything be made common' and that peasants were 'men formed in the likeness of their lords and should not be kept under like beasts'. In his *Letter to the Men of Essex* he quotes the contemporary poem *Piers Plowman*. The peasants were revolting against the Poll Tax. They stormed through the Gates of London and attacked the Lord Chancellor who had imposed it. The poem *Piers Plowman* has a dramatic account of Christ's harrowing of hell, where he descends on Good Friday and challenges Lucifer at the Gates of Hell:

> Thou art Doctor of Death, drink that thou madest!
> For I that am Lord of Life, love is my drink,
> And for that drink today, I died upon Earth.[180]

Incidentally, just over six centuries later, in the 1990 Poll Tax riots, which brought Thatcher down that same year, T-shirts and placards could be seen saying: AVENGE WAT TYLER! And in choosing to camp on Blackheath, the 2009 Climate Camp paid its respects to Wat Tyler, who led the peasants to camp there on their way into London.

During the English Revolution, on 1st April 1649 at about Easter time, Gerrard Winstanley led the Diggers, a group of poor and hungry people, to dig up and plant some land on St George's Hill in Surrey. He writes:

---

[180] William Langland, *The Vision of Piers Plowman,* passus XVIII, lines 365-7.

> The work we are going about is this, to dig up George's Hill and the waste ground thereabouts, and to sow corn; and to eat our bread together by the sweat of our brows. And the First Reason is this, that we may work together in righteousness and lay the foundation of making the Earth a Common Treasury for all, both rich and poor.[181]

He describes this work as 'Christ rising again in the sons and daughters'. It was a theological as well as a political action, and Winstanley's theology is not about salvation or liberation of one particular group; it is universalist:

> For the Earth with all her fruits of Corn, Cattle and such like, was made to be a Common Store-house of Livelihood to all Mankind, *friend and foe, without exception.*[182]

Christian language continued to be used down the centuries in the struggles of the English radical tradition. At the end of the nineteenth century, although he was not a Christian, the great harvest home banquet at the end of William Morris' *News from Nowhere* (1893) was surely inspired by the story of the Messianic banquet in the kingdom of God.

Like the seventeenth-century English Revolution, the twentieth-century Nicaraguan Revolution was a very *theological* revolution. Here is part of the Creed of the Nicaraguan *Peasant Mass*,[183] which echoes Winstanley's idea of the Diggers' action as 'Christ rising again in the sons and daughters':

---

181 Gerrard Winstanley, *A Declaration to the Powers of England and to all the Powers of the World...* (1649), in Gerrard Winstanley, *Selected Writings*, ed. Andrew Hopkins (Aporia Press, London 1989), p. 15.

182 *Declaration from the Poor Oppressed People of England* (1649), Winstanley, *Selected Writings,* p. 26.

183 Carlos Mejía Godoy, *Misa campesina,* translated by Dinah Livingstone, bilingual text, 2nd revised edition (Nicaragua Solidarity Campaign, London 2007).

I trust in you, comrade,
human Christ, Christ the worker,
death you've overcome.
Your fearful suffering
formed the new humanity
born for freedom.
You are rising now
each time we raise an arm
to defend the people
from profiteering dominion,
because you're living on the farm,
in the factory and in school,
your struggle goes on
and you're rising again.

When the Mass was sung in St Aloysius, Somers Town in London on 6th April 1986 (Low Sunday), by the composer, Carlos Mejía Godoy, and his group, Los de Palacagüina, with parts repeated in English, the right-wing Catholic paper, *The Universe,* had a shock-horror anti-communist headline: COMRADE CHRIST! In writing this Mass, Carlos Mejía was of course inspired by liberation theology, also one of the inspirations of the Sandinista Revolution that overthrew the Nicaraguan dictator Somoza in 1979.

One such liberation theologian, whom we have quoted in this book, is the Jesuit Jon Sobrino. He remains a Catholic theologian, who does not think God is a purely human creation. However, he does speak of 'God who has become history'.[184] And his agenda and that of his fellow liberation theologians is a *humanist* one: a decent life for everybody on Earth. He says God could not want something cruel *because* it is inhuman. The Doctors of Death still need to be challenged

---

[184] 'The Winds of Santo Domingo', p. 40.

at the Gates of Hell. Sobrino constantly denounces the 'idols of death', which operate even 'within the western Christian church... and those who claim to be defenders of this culture and Christian principles'. In fact, the Catholic church in Latin America and elsewhere sometimes looks like two opposing churches with two opposing Gods. There is the God of the conquistadors who persecuted and exterminated many of the indigenous people, the God of the rich and powerful today; and then the God of the poor. And of course now there is the growing power of the Evangelical New Christian Right in the USA and the God that told Bush to invade Iraq.

The church (churches) cannot be taken as a reliable moral guide. It has taught different things at different times (for example, now it does not promote the burning of heretics, although some twenty-first century bishops support the persecution, even execution, of gays). As noted above, now as ever, different churches or different sectors of a single church support different social classes or groups, and promote different, even opposing, views. Throughout its history the church has sometimes behaved with great cruelty, supported oppressors against the weak, the rich against the poor, blessed the guns of dictators, treated women abominably – including by a ban on contraception and abortion even when a woman's life is in danger – and has covered up the abuse of children. The list goes on.

Religion consists of poetic tales, part of the treasury we have inherited, some of it embodying valuable accumulated wisdom of our ancestors, some not. Religion is also about power and controlling access to supernatural beings as a way of keeping people in order. As Blake puts it: 'A system was formed, which some took advantage of, and enslaved the vulgar... thus began Priesthood.' We neither want nor need 'priests in black gowns' to control us. Behaviour cannot be judged on a god's divine say-so or the say-so of his priests – be they mitred archbishops or red-braced worshippers of Mammon in the City, who have always reminded me of the prophets of Baal that 'shrieked and capered and cut themselves with knives as is their custom'. The behaviour of humans (*and* their gods) has to be judged on humanist criteria. As with any other poetic material, we can sift the wisdom in religious tales, but their moral teaching has no supernatural authority and must be judged by humanist standards. The main criterion is *kindness* and the golden rule: 'Do as you would be done by.' A lot of the time we know perfectly well how to be kind; it's just a question of *doing* it. Or when things are more complex, we have to try to work them out together.

Neither can we say, as Don Cupitt does in *The Meaning of the West*,[185] that the West has now realised and embodied Christian principles. There have been great historical struggles, many, as we have seen, couched in Christian language, and for centuries the Christian story of the kingdom of God and the whole Christ as 'one body because we all share the same bread' have inspired and been a beacon in the ongoing struggle for a better life. In some ways we are now a more compassionate society and this compassion has been inspired by the Christian Grand Narrative: we don't stone people to death or cut off their hands or ears, we have a National Health Service, we profess that 'the poorest he hath a life to live' and that torture is abhorrent. Nevertheless, we still have a long way to go. Many people are poor or homeless in the West, as well as in developing countries, and we note that the richest Western country, the USA, *does* execute people, is only just beginning to have a national health insurance scheme (after tremendous and still virulent opposition), has the widest gap between the rich and poor of any Western nation, *does* torture people… In our

---

[185] Don Cupitt, *The Meaning of the West* (SCM Press, London 2008).

'special relationship' during the last thirty years British governments have aped the USA in some of its least humane policies, supported its wars and, as far as we can tell, been complicit, at least by silence, in its torturing of prisoners.

In their book *The Spirit Level*[186] social epidemiologists Richard Wilkinson and Kate Pickett point out that Western societies that are more unequal, that is, have the widest income gap between rich and poor, do worse in a whole range of ways, including infant mortality, mental illness, drug use, obesity, literacy, social mobility, public trust, homicide and imprisonment rates. The country with the widest income gap, the USA, does worst on all these indicators. The authors show that since 1979 when Margaret Thatcher's Conservative government came to power with her admiration for President Reagan and US neoliberal policies, followed by a New Labour government with similar inclinations, Britain has deteriorated in the direction of the USA. We note also that the USA is probably the most religious of rich Western societies. There is no room for complacency.

Because, historically, the church has formally proclaimed the gospel of the reign of God as good news for the poor, yet done the very opposite in all kinds of ways, taking a whole range of different positions and supporting a whole range of worldly powers, particularly its own, it is urgent that it should acknowledge itself *and* its changing God to be a fallible human creation. Apart from fundamentalists (who, incidentally, sometimes have additional whimsical fancies, such as that their dead cats are waiting for them in heaven), I think that probably many clergy already do know this, but keep quiet about it so as not to shock their congregation, and many of

---

[186] Richard Wilkinson and Kate Pickett, *The Spirit Level* (revised pbk edition, Penguin, London 2010).

the congregation likewise keep mum so as not to disappoint the clergy: 'It would be rude to the parson.'

In this conflict between 'kind' and 'unkind' – 'death and life in strange strife': *mors et vita duello conflixere mirando,* as the ancient Easter hymn has it – if the church is to retain any credibility at all, it *must* opt for the spirit of kindness (with or without a capital letter) and *act* kindly. It must be faithful to the gospel of the kingdom. If the church stopped claiming privileged access to supernatural beings and acknowledged that we had created these ourselves, then it would be easier for it to make common cause with fellow human beings in the great task of the making of a humankind that *is* kind, a humanity that *is* humane.

As we have seen, we create God(s) by the poetic trope of supernaturalisation of cosmic powers and of forces – actual or potential – in ourselves. For the latter, God can be seen as an 'emergent property' in us. We create God as a blueprint for the making of humanity. As well as Word, this God we have created is Spirit, the spirit of kindness, which it behoves a humane humanity to 'breathe' and activate. As in the Trinity the Word *speaks* the Father, we humans can *speak* our planet and our cosmos, as well as recalling, re-voicing the fathers and mothers that begat us. The Word also speaks *itself* and together (all the energy of the cosmos that created us, and all our human conscious powers) we can pour into love.

If the Word with its spirit of kindness can only emerge in *us*, then it becomes *our* responsibility to act and save our species and our planet. Although we have seen a growing 'global consciousness', we do not see our leaders getting it together very well, for example, at the 2009 Climate Change Conference in Copenhagen. So perhaps we must conclude that we have not yet 'emerged' very far and if we don't get our act together, we may not have much time left to emerge much further. How the Grand Narrative ends is up to us.

Present!

In their 'quest for the historical Jesus' some writers hold that he was a purely secular moral teacher who taught that we should be kind to one another, and that the whole Christ Epic should be discarded as an 'accretion'. Jesus did teach that we should be kind to one another, though it is hard to imagine how any teacher born into the cultural context he was would be 'purely secular'. Jesus taught in parables and his teaching of the coming reign of God is a parable or story of the coming of a just society on Earth. We could call it a dream – an 'enabling' dream – or perhaps 'it may be called a vision rather than a dream'. At the very end of *News from Nowhere*, Ellen, the wise and beautiful woman from Guest's dream of the future, retreats with the final words:

> Go on living while you may, striving with whatsoever pain and labour needs must be, to build up little by little the new day of fellowship, and rest, and happiness.

Guest, who has now woken 'in his bed in dingy Hammersmith', responds:

> Yes surely! and if others can see it as I have seen it, then it may be called a vision rather than a dream.

As we have seen in chapter 3, Jesus' preaching of the kingdom is one 'take' on the Christian Grand Narrative of human fulfilment. The Christ Epic, with its images of the body of Christ, bridegroom and bride, the beautiful city, is another. Then, beginning from the Prologue to John's Gospel, we have the later developed theology of the Incarnate Word. If we have been given all this richness, why not ponder it all?

The church should fully acknowledge (an acknowledgment which, at present, seems very unlikely) that this Grand Narrative and the supernatural beings in it are creations of the human poetic genius, albeit creations of the utmost importance. First, let the church behave kindly, which may require great bravery in bearing witness and speaking out against 'the oppressor's wrong, the proud man's contumely' – when Archbishop Romero did this he was shot dead at Mass. Then let the church celebrate the Incarnate Word. That is to say, keep proclaiming, playing the gospel, speaking, performing the Word, the great Christian epic of human salvation, liberation, fulfilment – go on telling the stories, singing its magnificent music, reading out the ancient texts and reflecting on them, as well as new poetry, new music, new insights. Let it work out how to go on enacting the liturgy with 'poetic faith', especially the drama of incarnation at Christmas and crucifixion and resurrection at Easter, keeping Christ present in a Grand Narrative that has not yet reached its conclusion, the coming of the kingdom, the reign of kindness. For Jesus himself 'the final reality was not simply "God" but "the kingdom of God".'[187]

As it goes on breaking bread and sharing the wine cup of the Eucharist 'in memory of me', let the church keep Christ present both in the symbolic bread and wine and in the ceremony of sharing it, by which the community *becomes* the body of Christ, comes together *as* the body of Christ. Liturgy and ritual are performative. A sacrament 'effects what it signifies' and the Eucharist is a symbolic – sacramental – play or performance with audience participation. It also recalls

---

[187] *Jesus,* p. 68, quoted on page 89 in the section on 'The Kingdom of God'.

names of Christians from the past and often celebrates a saint's day. The 'communion of saints' includes all those, past and present, who have been members of Christ's body and looks forward to the future, 'the measure of the stature of the fullness of Christ'. Like the reign of God, the body of Christ is a metaphor or parable of the making of humanity on Earth, which the eucharistic play symbolically presents. It is an invitation to love one another, looking forward to 'the new day of fellowship and rest and happiness'. In that sense it has everything to play for:

> You must sit down, says Love, and taste my meat.
> So I did sit and eat.[188]

However, the church should remember that it does not *own* the Christian Grand Narrative, any more than the Royal Shakespeare Company owns Shakespeare's plays. Jesus Christ is out of copyright. He himself said: 'For where two or three are gathered in my name, I am there among them.'[189] The whole New Testament, Jesus' preaching of the reign of God and the Christ Epic are now part of our common human treasury; they belong to us all. As we have seen, in this story, although the 'body of Christ' is, firstly, the church, it is potentially the whole of humanity, an epic project of human fulfilment. That is a project of passionate concern to us all, which can also be expressed in many other stories and poems.

Nevertheless, there is a price to be paid if the church is to retain credibility in its ceremonies and liturgy. We saw that in each version of the Christian Grand Narrative there is a 'scandal'. In Jesus' preaching of the kingdom, the scandal is that it belongs first and foremost to the poor and it is very hard for the rich to enter it. The scandal of the body of Christ

---

[188] These are the final lines of George Herbert's poem 'Love'.
[189] Mt 18: 20.

is that that body was *broken*. The scandal of the theology of the Incarnate Word is the 'sharing of properties', that what is said of the human Christ can be said of God, because Christ is one person, *the same, the same, the same*. So we can say God *suffered*. Poor, broken, suffering. The church hierarchy will be scandalised, even appalled, at what is now required of it: that is, to acknowledge that *because* the whole supernatural realm is a human creation, it must renounce its claim to divine authority and the privileges that go with it. The church is the Jesus Christ Society. Let it 'come down to the place just right', let it 'empty itself' into humanity.

In Latin America, they honour their heroes and martyrs by calling out their names in a ceremony – at Mass perhaps – and the people reply: *Present!* as in a roll call. At the demonstration outside the House of Lords when the Pinochet extradition case was being tried, you could hear them calling out the name of Chile's elected socialist president, Allende, who died in Pinochet's bloody coup that inaugurated his reign of torture and mass murder. They were shouting: *¡Se siente, se siente. Allende está presente!*: We sense it, we sense it. Allende is present!'

In choosing to camp on Blackheath, we noted, the 2009 Climate Camp paid its respects to Wat Tyler: *Wat Tyler: Present!* I often walk through London and feel the presence of great spirits from our own radical tradition. In Old St Pancras churchyard I stand by Wollstonecraft's tomb: *Mary Wollstonecraft: Present!* In Bunhill Fields I nod to Blake: *William Blake: Present!* And to Bunyan with his Great-Heart: *John Bunyan: Present!* In St Giles Cripplegate I bow to Milton: *John Milton: Present!* And I hear his words ringing in my ear, what he would have to say to greedy, fraudulent MPs and bankers bagging big bonuses willy nilly:

Help us to save free conscience from the paw
of hireling wolves whose gospel is their maw!

We honour our cultural ancestors, as the liturgy celebrates the communion of saints and builds up the body of Christ. The English radical tradition has strong Christian roots, deep in the Christian Grand Narrative. The 'body of Christ' is a metaphor for a fulfilled humanity, *habeas corpus* in the full sense for all. So as in the Eucharist, I say, thankfully: *Jesus Christ: Present!*

Kindness and Poetry

Kindness is essential but neither can we do without poetry, music and ritual. As we saw in chapter 1, poetic concentration is increased by the use of symbolic language, including supernaturalisation. A people is impoverished and its poetry becomes thinner if they lose their theology and poetic tales (of course, religious stories are just part of our common treasury, but these are what the body of this book has focused on). It is important both to acknowledge these for what they are – human creations – and to keep them active in an abundant and kindly imaginative life. To me it seems puritanical and repressive for a religious ceremony just to sit around in silence, boasting that 'we have no theology'. Rather than no theology, we could call this *poor* theology, trying to 'spiritualise' the word by disembodying and privatising it as much as possible.

Kindness matters most and the greatest of all gifts is love. That is true for everyone. Ethics (as well as science) are very important but not enough; we need poetry. As Mary Wollstonecraft put it: 'Imagination is the true fire stolen from heaven that renders men social by expanding their hearts.' And as we said in chapter 1, here poetry is a paradigm for every kind of knowing *how to* that becomes an art, every grace that is 'pure poetry'. We saw that children start using symbolic language almost as soon as they learn to talk at all. And it is constantly amazing how early human beings not only learn to make tools and vessels but to decorate them, not only live in caves but paint murals on them, not only speak but make poems and songs. Poetry is not a luxury added on when we become better educated. Even the most primitive societies are awash with it, as well as singing and dancing; in fact, it is more 'civilised' people who are sometimes in danger of losing the power of poetry.

The classic objective of secular humanism is 'the cultivation of a rational and humane way of life'. A rational way of life on its own is a very restricted form of humanity. It excludes too much of our consciousness, not to mention our emerging unconscious, our terrors, our hopes and dreams, what we feel and make of living on Earth and our relationship to the whole vast cosmos. These are what 'poetic tales', including religious stories, abundantly articulate. Reason matters but so do beauty and gusto, the oomph of life. So do meaning and feeling. Knowledge is useful, kindness is vital but to a fully humane humanity, poetry is also a necessity. That is the *kind* of creature humans are. A society in which everyone was well lodged, clothed and fed, but which suppressed poetry (or the other arts) would not be kind. At the end of John Heath-Stubbs' poem 'Plato and the Waters of the Flood', after Plato has expelled the poets, the question surges unstoppably:

When will you rise again,
Ten-horned, seven-headed seraphim,
Out of your abyss,
Against the beautiful Republic –
Nor tamed by Plato's kiss?

That was why, immediately after the triumph of the Nicaraguan Revolution on 19th July 1979, the Sandinistas not only began introducing measures to tackle health, literacy, land titles and other urgent social problems (they ran an international-prize-winning literacy campaign and eradicated polio), but in an impoverished and battered country (the falling dictator had bombed his own capital) they set up poetry workshops all over the country. The Minister of Culture, Ernesto Cardenal, was a famous poet and Catholic priest. Graffiti appeared on walls: 'The triumph of the Revolution is the triumph of poetry.'

They were an inspiration to people all over the world.[190] We want a world of justice and peace, which is also a world of abundant life. We want human lives to be abundant, not only with love, but with everything that makes for the richness of humanity, all the magnificent paintings and sculpture, all the beautiful weaving, knitting, sewing and embroidery, all the song and dance, music and poetry and all the rest. It is true, humans cannot live by bread alone; that would not be a human life.

It is vital to defend with Keats 'the holiness of the heart's affections and the truth of imagination'. We are poetic animals, who can not only speak ourselves but our world. We are the voice of the planet, the universe. If the universe has other voices, we have not yet heard them.

Blake's poem 'Auguries of Innocence' begins:

> To see a world in a grain of sand
> And a heaven in a wild flower,

---

[190] At the time I was running a poetry workshop in Camden as an ILEA (Inner London Education Authority) evening class. US President Reagan was determined to smash the Nicaraguan Revolution, which posed 'the threat of a good example'. With similar venom, Reagan's admirer Margaret Thatcher abolished the ILEA.

Hold infinity in the palm of your hand
And eternity in an hour.

That is the most complete form of poetic 'thickening', and reminds us of the philosopher Boethius' famous definition of eternity: *interminabilis vitae tota simul et perfecta possessio.* Eternity is the perfect possession *all at once* of everlasting life. Blake, of course, was no other-worldly mystic and never forgets for a moment that kindness matters most. The lines immediately following the ones quoted above from his 'Auguries of Innocence' are:

A robin redbreast in a cage
Puts all heaven in a rage.

If we think of the divine as a potential in us, we can think of our word, our wisdom, our *logosofia,* aspiring poetically (at least at times) to this *tota simul* condition of eternity, *and* that wisdom then breathing love. But as we have seen, poetry deals in intractable particularity. Unless it is fully grounded, fleshed out, its aspirations fail. To be effective, *logosofia* must come down to Earth. Likewise, love and kindness – think of mothering – often involve a lot of hard work. Humanity in the fullest sense is poetry and kindness, incarnate word and deed.

There is so much more that could be said about these things that if it were all written down, I suppose that the world itself could not contain the books that would be written.

Index

Books of the Bible are shown in italics.